HOW TO TALK TO ANYONE

HOW TO MASTER SMALL TALK SO YOU CAN TALK TO STRANGERS, WIN FRIENDS, AND INFLUENCE PEOPLE

DYLAN WINTON

ANNUS MIRABILIS
PUBLISHING

© Copyright 2024 Dylan Winton - All rights reserved.

The content contained within this book may not be reproduced, duplicated, or transmitted without direct written permission from the author or the publisher.

Under no circumstances will any blame or legal responsibility be held against the publisher, or author, for any damages, reparation, or monetary loss due to the information contained within this book. Either directly or indirectly.

Legal Notice

This book is copyright protected. This book is only for personal use. You cannot amend, distribute, sell, use, quote or paraphrase any part, or the content within this book, without the consent of the author or publisher.

Disclaimer Notice

Please note the information contained within this document is for educational and entertainment purposes only. All effort has been executed to present accurate, up to date, and reliable, complete information. No warranties of any kind are declared or implied. Readers acknowledge that the author is not engaging in the rendering of legal, financial, medical or professional advice. The content within this book has been derived from various sources. Please consult a licensed professional before attempting any techniques outlined in this book.

By reading this document, the reader agrees that under no circumstances is the author responsible for any losses, direct or indirect, which are incurred as a result of the use of the information contained within this document, including, but not limited to, — errors, omissions, or inaccuracies.

CONTENTS

Introduction   v

1. Making a Memorable First Impression   1
2. Captivating Attention in Conversations   13
3. Mastering Body Language   24
4. Rapid Rapport-Building Techniques   35
5. Working a Room Like a Pro   47
6. Overcoming Conversation Challenges   59
7. Encouraging Openness in Others   72
8. Becoming a Conversation Magnet   84
9. Mastering Digital Communication   95

Conclusion   107

INTRODUCTION

Have you ever met someone who seems to be a natural conversationalist? There are some people in this world who can talk to anyone about anything. Whether at a business meeting or a social gathering, these types of people know how to get and keep a conversation flowing. Maybe you don't think you're that type of person. Maybe you don't think you have what it takes to break out of your shell and make new connections. Well, this guide will show you you're wrong!

Mastering the art of small talk is no easy task, but it's not impossible. While it's true that there are some people who are more extroverted than others or who excel in the gift of gab, even the most outgoing folks aren't born conversationalists. Some people are shy or simply don't have the tools needed to get a conversation off the ground. Learning to talk to others is an acquired skill, one that takes lots of trial, error, and real-world practice.

This book isn't just about learning to talk to anyone; it's about creating connections. We create connections with others by asking questions, showing interest in them, and being actively engaged. Having a meaningful conversation with someone is just as much about listening as it is about talking. The journey from a simple "hello" to making meaningful connections begins here.

WHY IS COMMUNICATION IMPORTANT?

In so many relationships, whether business or personal, the root of many problems boils down to a lack of communication or miscommunication. Being able to accurately deliver information or tell people your needs and feelings is an important life skill for everyone to learn. Whether you need to advocate for yourself, or simply want to make some new friends, saying what you mean in a clear, concise, and understandable way is essential.

The purpose of this book is to give you the tools and confidence you need to get out there and start talking. Communicating is a part of being human, and in our digital age, our in-person social skills have become rusty or been lost altogether for many of us. The world is full of many different people, all with different personalities, but we all have one thing in common — the desire to connect.

The advice in this guide is not one size fits all. Those with certain disorders like autism or ADHD may require additional support when it comes to overcoming conversation hurdles. Please take the advice in this guide as just that — a guide. There's always more than one way to reach a destination, so certain conversational tactics might not work for every person in every case. Furthermore, some people just might not be in the mood to talk or socialize, and that's okay too! Not everyone will be receptive when it comes to making small talk, but that won't be a reflection of you. Different people meet different social milestones at their own pace, and being mindful of that is a non-verbal communication that shows respect.

WHAT'S INSIDE

This guide is broken down into easily digestible, step-by-step sections. At the end of each section, you'll have a mission to complete to put those steps in action and practice what you've learned. Once you've mastered one section or chapter, you can move on to the next at your own pace.

Here are the elements we will cover in this guide:

First Impressions

You only get one! First impressions offer a brief window of time for people to form an initial opinion of you. From your appearance to your body language, we'll show you the best ways to present yourself from the start.

Captivating Your Audience

Once you've got someone's attention, how do you keep it? We'll cover everything from storytelling tips and active listening to the art of asking questions, all to help you forge genuine connections with others.

Body Language

Tell them everything they need to know without saying a word. This section will teach you how to master the way you carry yourself and your body language during conversations. From gestures and facial expressions to body mirroring, you'll learn how to be mindful of your actions so that your body and your words align.

Building Rapport

Learn to find common ground and bond with others through empathy and validation. This chapter is designed to help you turn fleeting interactions into lasting connections through shared experiences and more. You'll also learn how to adjust your communication styles for those who may not be as skilled at expressing themselves.

Working the Room

Stepping into a room of strangers can be scary, but not if you know how to navigate the space. We'll show you how to make a memorable entrance, leverage networking strategies and create a lasting impression on associates and peers.

Overcoming Challenges

Even the most skilled communicator encounters conversational roadblocks. From awkward silences to language barriers and cultural differences, there are many challenges that can occur during communication. We'll outline some of the most common situations, from handling difficult conversations to recovering from conversational errors.

Encouraging Others

It takes two to have a conversation, and sometimes, coaxing the other person to open up is part of the battle. We'll show you how to create a safe space for others, build trust and practice empathetic listening, all while respecting each others' boundaries. This section is about encouraging conversation — not forcing it.

Conversational Magnet

Learn how to naturally be more charismatic and make every interaction more interesting. Use humor and wit to cultivate curiosity and leave a lasting impression that will encourage people to want to speak with you again and again.

Communicating Online

From text messages to emails, learning how to effectively communicate online is an essential 21st century skill. We'll discuss online messaging etiquette, how to create impactful social media interactions, video calls and more.

At the end of each section, you'll have the opportunity to participate in a challenge to put the skills you've learned to the test. We'll give you a task designed to help you improve your communication skills and build your confidence in the real world. Complete these challenges at your own pace, and feel free to go back and practice as often as you need to until you feel like you've mastered each skill.

Like most folks, I wasn't born with the ability to comfortably talk to strangers. Even though I enjoy meeting new people, I can be shy in certain situations. I identify as an introvert and used to find it difficult to open up, especially when I felt intimidated or anxious. I've also suffered from my own personal setbacks due to miscommunication with friends and romantic partners. When it comes to communication, learning to see the whole picture and practicing the skills outlined in this guide have helped me in countless ways. I feel more confident now when I introduce myself to others and can engage more authentically, and I hope this guide will help you in the same way.

Thank you for coming along on this journey with me as we learn how to master the art of small talk, making friends and influencing others!

1

MAKING A MEMORABLE FIRST IMPRESSION

"You never get a second chance to make a first impression."

— WILL ROGERS

Within the first seven seconds of meeting another person, they often decide what kind of person you are. From the expression on your face to the clothes you wear, how you look and present yourself is very important when you first meet someone. Let's make sure their initial assumptions about you are right!

It's easy to get off on the wrong foot, and sometimes rebounding from a bad first impression can be nearly impossible. As most of us have seen, many romantic comedies start this way, with the two leads taking one look at each other and assuming the worst. It's easy to make a bad impression if you're having a bad day, whether you're not feeling well or you spilled coffee down the front of your shirt. But don't worry! In Chapter 6: Overcoming Conversation Challenges, we'll show you how to recover from a bad first impression.

For now, we're going to focus on making sure you always present yourself in a way that results in a great first impression. Read on and we'll discover the science behind first impressions, appearance and attire tips, body language basics, the art of introduction and more. We'll also share some easy to remember opening lines and icebreakers so you can start up a successful conversation every time.

THE POWER OF FIRST IMPRESSIONS

While we've all heard the saying, "Don't judge a book by its cover," unfortunately, that's not the reality when it comes to our reaction to first impressions. When we meet someone for the first time, our brains process an abundance of information, right down to the most minute details. First impressions are powerful, and can be the deciding factor in whether or not someone wants to approach you or engage with you in conversation. Humans aren't being judgmental on purpose…it's just how we're built! Our initial impression of someone is rooted in psychology and physiology, and can influence how you are viewed and treated by someone for a very long time.

Judging someone quickly is intrinsically linked to survival. From an evolutionary perspective, our ancestors had to be able to decide whether to welcome strangers or run from them, and this knee-jerk reaction still manifests in first impressions today. In fact, our brains are biologically hard-wired to quickly decide if someone is a friend or a foe based on existing biases and information collection.

In psychology, first impressions are based on a variety of factors, including physical appearance, posture, age, attire, race, language, accent, gender and voice. We are socially conditioned to create a mental picture of someone based on the information we are taught or have learned from real life experiences. If someone is attractive or appears to be trustworthy, the speed in which the average person will want to engage with them will likely increase. The University of York even released a study in 2014 reporting that facial features associated with youthfulness and attractiveness correlated with how approachable a person seems.

Neuroscience shows that we process information about others through our prefrontal cortex. This information, such as facial features and expressions, is directly tied to our initial impression of a person. In some studies, people tended to form more negative opinions to faces that showed negative emotions than they did to faces with neutral expressions. This is why the advice to smile when you first meet someone is so important.

Often, stories of first meetings are tied to romance. Consider the most infamous of all first impressions in romance films in *When Harry Met Sally*. Their first impressions of each other were terrible! But through icebreakers and conversation, they eventually saw eye-to-eye and maintained a rapport that turned into romance. Making a memorable first impression isn't always tied to romance, of course. However, if you are trying to talk to a prospective romantic partner, all the advice in this guide will work for you as well.

First impressions are long-lasting and can set the foundation for every interaction we have with someone. People can rely on limited or misleading information to draw conclusions about you, and this can lead to broad implications or poor decisions down the road. By taking control and being conscious of the impression you give to others, you're taking the reins and guiding others to form a favorable opinion of you. Read on and we'll explore some of the key ways you can influence others to see you in a positive light before you even say "hello."

APPEARANCE AND ATTIRE

It's thought that around 69% of people will form a first impression of you before you even have a chance to speak. When it comes to making a first impression, appearances can be everything. Thankfully, one of the easiest things we can control when it comes to the way others perceive us is our appearance and attire. What you wear and how you groom yourself play a major role in the way people think about you, not just for first impressions, but all the time. How you wear your hair, your level of cleanliness, the style and care you take in your clothing and even the way you smell can impact the way someone perceives you.

Grooming and clothing have long been a nonverbal indicator to others about who you are. The way you present yourself through clothing, hairstyle and makeup can tell others your social class, financial status, religious beliefs and more. However, it isn't always easy to balance our personal style with situational appropriateness. Personal style is just that — personal. It will be up to you to decide which parts of your personality you want to let shine through when creating a first impression.

When it comes to wardrobe, whatever you choose to wear should always be neat, clean and appropriately tailored or fitted for your shape. Remember to choose clothing that makes you feel comfortable, or else your discomfort will show in your body language. It's more important to wear clothes that make you feel confident and comfortable than to wear restrictive clothes or clothes that don't suit you simply to fit in. Natural, breathable fabrics like cotton are always excellent choices for sweaty situations, while clothes made from wrinkle-resistant polyester are ideal for professional settings.

Another thing to keep in mind is the color of clothing you wear. Whether we realize it or not, the colors that we present ourselves in can subconsciously influence the way others perceive us. Certain patterns or colors can be off-putting in certain social situations. For example, no one other than the bride should be wearing white to a wedding. Some colors can even have a biological effect on the viewer. Red, for example, has been tied to increased heart rate (cite). Check out the quick guide below to see which colors you may want to consider when picking out your first impression ensembles.

White - neutral, inviting
Black - powerful, serious, intelligent, mysterious
Red - passion, aggression, sexuality, romance
Blue - peace, cooperation, calm, friendliness, honesty
Yellow - awareness, optimism, confidence, creativity
Green - happiness, peace
Purple - royalty, sophistication, creativity, joy
Pink - warmth, friendliness, femininity
Orange - energy, enthusiasm, creativity, warmth

Now that you have a basic understanding of how what you wear and how you groom yourself affects the perception of others, you can confidently present yourself in any situation. Here's a quick checklist to consider before you head out the door to that next meeting or social gathering.

Cleanliness - Shower, shave, dental care, nail care. Details matter!
Hair - Combed, clean, styled. Is it time for a trim?
Scent - Fresh breath? Stinky bits deodorized?
Clothes - Are your clothes clean? Neat? Free of stains and holes? Are they comfortable and appropriate for the event/meeting/social situation?

Ready to go? Great! Dressing for success is the first step when it comes to making a great first impression.

BODY LANGUAGE BASICS

When it comes to body language, reading people is like reading a book. Whether we know it or not, our body language can give away how we feel at any given moment. In fact, forensic psychologists are trained to read the body language of criminal suspects to help evaluate whether they might be lying or not. Learning how to present yourself with body language and decode the non-verbal cues of others is an essential communication skill that can be simple to learn.

When it comes to decoding non-verbal cues, some gestures and body positions are more obvious to detect than others. If someone is hugging their arms to their chest and avoiding eye contact, they may be feeling shy or uncomfortable. However, if a person is facing you with their arms relaxed, and making direct eye contact, they are likely interested in engaging in conversation with you.

Our body language when we first encounter someone can have a significant impact on whether or not they want to speak with us. If you rush up to a stranger and display aggressive, tense body language, that person may naturally turn away from you. However, if you approach someone in a relaxed, friendly manner, you'll have a much better chance at striking up a conversation. Facial expressions are also very important to consider when meeting someone new, which is why it's important that you feel comfortable in what you wear. A too-tight pair of shoes can cause pain that negatively affects your expression, even if you're smiling. When meeting new people, a genuine smile and neutral expression are best.

Another way to utilize body language and build rapport is to mirror the other person's body posture. This is a subtle, subconscious way to let someone know that you are actively engaged with them. For example, if the person you are conversing with has their arms crossed in front of them, slowly cross your own arms as you speak. This mirroring can help them feel a little more at ease and lead to a better conversation.

When we are nervous, our body language tends to show it in ways that we may not realize. Here are a few body language mistakes to avoid when you are trying to engage with someone new:

- Weak handshake
- Crossing your arms
- Not smiling
- Leaning back or away
- Nervous gestures
- No eye contact/intense eye contact
- Slouching/poor posture
- Excessive nodding

Some of these body language no-no's come from bad habits or from simply being unaware of how we carry ourselves. The best way to practice breaking these bad habits is in front of a mirror or with a friend or partner. Create a mock conversation and take note of your posture, your facial expression, and any nervous gestures you may make. You can also try this out in public, during a walk in the park as you pass strangers or at the grocery store. Think about how you present your outward self as you go about your day. You may be surprised to find that you fidget or slouch or nod more than you thought!

THE ART OF THE INTRODUCTION

Introducing yourself to someone new is an art form all in itself. If you are too timid, you might not get the other person's attention. If you come on too strong, your interaction may be off-putting. It is crucial to strike a balance somewhere in between these two and find that sweet spot when it comes to meeting new people. There are many things to consider when greeting someone new, from cultural differences to physical contact preferences. Before you even say "hello," take some of these tips to heart and make sure you start off on the right foot.

Make It Memorable: The first step to crafting a memorable self-introduction is learning to remember names. Remembering someone's name is an excellent way to subconsciously let that person know that you are genuinely interested in them. When you are speaking to them, be sure to use their name when you greet them and again when you part. I recently met a new colleague at an event and wanted to be sure I remembered their name. It turns out, they share the name of one of my favorite actors (Luke). Now, each time I interact with that person, I make sure to assign the mental picture of that actor to them and — bingo! I remember their name every time.

Handshake Do's and Don'ts: Handshakes can be tricky. This traditional greeting may seem too formal for certain interactions or too intrusive for those who prefer not to have physical contact. Not everyone wants to shake hands and that's okay, especially those who are immunocompromised. It is okay to offer a fist bump or elbow bump in lieu of a handshake, or politely decline contact at all. Handshakes can be a powerful greeting when meeting new clients, business partners, or in social situations, so be sure to practice good hygiene and always greet a new person with clean, sanitized hands.

When shaking hands, be sure to use your dominant hand and avoid standing too close. Maintain comfortable eye contact as you grip your new acquaintance's hand with the same pressure you would a door handle. Use a firm, but gentle grip that's not too tight and not too loose, and never with clammy hands. Some folks, like small children or elderly persons may require a lighter touch, so be sure to adjust the strength of your handshake to the individual. In some cultures, handshake greetings can vary and even include kisses, hugs or bowing. If you know you'll be meeting someone for the first time from a different cultural background than you, the polite thing to do is research their customs beforehand. Greeting a person in a way that makes them comfortable is the best kind of first impression anyone can make.

Practice at Home: Ask a partner or friend to greet you in a mock handshake scenario. Smile, maintain comfortable eye-contact and approach them at an appropriate distance. Offer a firm, comfortable handshake without letting your grip linger, and ask your partner for feedback. How did you do?

OPENING LINES AND ICEBREAKERS

So you've greeted a new acquaintance. You've exchanged names, said hello and shaken hands. Now what? Coming up with a good opening line or icebreaker is the next step in getting that conversation flowing. Below are a few great opening lines anyone can use.

Ask a Question: Is the person wearing an interesting item of clothing or jewelry? Ask them about it! Are you at an event? Ask them how they are enjoying it. So long as you keep your tone friendly, asking questions can show genuine interest and lead to other questions or discovery of shared interests.

Ask for Information: Even if you already know the answer, asking someone for information is a great way to build rapport. If you are at a business meeting, something as simple as "Do you know who will be speaking next?" is a great way to open the door to easy conversation.

Comment on Something Nice: While it may seem cliche to talk about the weather, if it's an unusually nice day, feel free to comment on it. If you recently saw a new film that you liked or if your favorite sports team won, you might bring that up, as well. These ice breakers are great low-stakes ways to discover similar interests.

Ask Their Opinion: When you ask someone for their opinion, it shows that you value what they have to say. Be sure to choose a topic that is relevant to the situation. For example, if you're at a bar, ask them if they're regulars or what type of alcoholic beverage they enjoy.

When it comes to choosing your opening line, context is key. Be sure to "read the room" and make sure that your questions or conversational topics are appropriate. If you meet a new person at a funeral, it's probably not be the best time to crack a joke, for example. Don't encourage someone new to share anything too personal or get too physically close. If you remain genuine and respectful, your introductions will land every time.

Now that you've gotten your new acquaintance to open up a bit, you can continue to chip away and break the ice. At this stage, you can become a little more personal with your questions. However, there's a point where you can become too personal, too imposing, or too silly, so knowing how far to go is important. A successful icebreaker can help you learn more about a new person and be the starting point in transitioning from acquaintance to friend.

Successful Ice Breakers:

- Where are you from?
- What school did you go to?
- Share a photo from your phone (be careful you don't show something too personal!)
- Share career or hobby interests
- Ask about pets, kids or family

Unsuccessful Ice Breakers:

- Rude jokes
- Pranks
- Asking "Have you ever" or "Two truths and a lie" questions (these can become too personal)
- Flirting (not a good idea in business situations)
- Anything that requires physical touch

Now it's time to practice! Do you have a happy hour, wedding or other social event coming up? Use these low-stakes events as an opportunity to practice chatting up new folks. Write down a few lines or icebreaker topics ahead of time and practice on the way there so when it's time to meet someone new, your conversation will be organic and relaxed.

YOUR MISSION

Make a memorable first impression. This week, try to put everything in this chapter into practice and meet someone new. Start by picking out a comfortable outfit that fits your personality and the occasion at which you want to wear it. Make sure you're well groomed and relaxed, with your handshake perfected and opening lines at the ready. Climb out of your shell and introduce yourself to at least one new person using the tips we've just covered.

You've got this!

2

CAPTIVATING ATTENTION IN CONVERSATIONS

Great conversation is not just about what you say, but how you listen and respond. It's the difference between a forgettable encounter and an unforgettable connection. If your goal is to capture someone's attention and keep it, you'll need to become an engaging storyteller. Author Christopher Hitchens was one such famed storyteller. Hitchens, or "Hitch" as he was affectionately known, was revered for his skills as a conversationalist. He could effortlessly engage with others on a variety of topics, from religion and politics, to history and beyond, and confidently won over his conversational partners with jokes and innate charm.

There could only be one Hitch, but his successful public speaking methods can be taught to almost anyone. There is much that can be learned from observing successful conversationalists, so find a celebrity or public figure you admire who is gifted in gab and look for ways to apply their methods in your own encounters. Read on to discover some of the methods that successful storytellers use to keep their new acquaintances and friends entertained and engaged.

ENGAGING STORYTELLING

Telling a story or holding a conversation in an engaging way isn't always a walk in the park. Have you ever had someone tell you about their dream, or about a vacation or something that happened to them in a meandering way? You'll lose your listeners' attention fast if they aren't interested in what you have to say. Knowing the elements of a captivating story is a surefire way to make sure you catch and hold anyone's interest.

The Elements of a Captivating Story

Much like writing a book, telling a story in person is an art. If you're nervous, or don't think the person you're speaking to is interested, your story might not be very good. However, as with the rest of these communication skills, learning the elements to storytelling will help you naturally be better at it. Check out these key elements of a captivating story and soon you'll have your new acquaintances hanging on to your every word!

Know Your Audience: Before you go to a business meeting or event, prepare a story that would naturally engage the people there. Are you going to a wedding for an old friend? Think about an amusing and positive story about your friend to share with the other wedding guests.

Get Personal: But not too personal! Share a positive or interesting detail about yourself during a story that will make your listener smile. Take care to balance your personal anecdotes with questions about your listener; no one appreciates people who only talk about themselves!

Use Visuals: Is there something unusual about the story you're telling that would stand out? A silly cat, or someone wearing something wacky? Use those kinds of details to create amusing visuals your audience will want to know more about and won't forget.

Build Suspense and Intrigue: Keep your listener hooked! Cliffhangers will have them hanging on the edge of their seat, wanting to know what happens next. To effectively build suspense, don't reveal too much information all at once. Slowly reveal details, like breadcrumbs on a path, and they'll follow your conversation to the end.

Use Humor Effectively: Avoid rude jokes, but feel free to let your comedic side shine. Talk about something funny that happened to you or relate an amusing situation you witnessed. Much like building suspense, save the punchline for the end so they'll wait for it. After your joke lands, be sure to leave a little space for laughter.

Put your newfound storytelling skills into practice! Kids and pets make great sounding boards for story time, or you could simply record yourself speaking out loud. Once you've got your storytelling methods down, grab a friend, tell them a story and ask for their opinion. Watch their body language, facial expressions and other visual cues as you speak to see if they remain engaged. With a little practice, any time can be story time!

ACTIVE LISTENING SKILLS

Have you ever been in a meeting, lecture or social situation in which you were supposed to be listening to someone speak but instead found your thoughts wandering? It's okay, you're not alone! Many folks, for example, those with ADHD, struggle with active listening. The good news is that a few exercises and techniques can help you become a better active listener.

Active listening is very important when it comes to making a first impression or meeting someone new. This style of communication shows that you're locked into the conversation and truly listening, not just hearing what the other person has to say. When we communicate with one another, we exhibit visual and subconscious clues that indicate whether or not we're listening. This can include eye contact, head nodding, and engaged body language. Knowing these key active listening skills can help you avoid embarrassing communication mistakes that may cost you a new business partner or friend.

Hearing vs. Listening: Hearing is physiological; our bodies process and attend to the sound within an environment. Listening, on the other hand, is a concentrated and focused way to understand a message. When people are talking, take a moment to consider whether you're actually listening to them, or if you're just hearing them speak.

Showing Attentiveness: In addition to maintaining eye contact and nodding, be sure to "check in" while someone is speaking to show you're paying attention. Brief affirmations like "I know" or "I see" can help the speaker feel like you're keeping up with the conversation.

Paraphrasing: This one is easy, and will help you get back into the conversation if you find yourself zoning out. Paraphrasing means simply repeating in your own words what the person said to you to confirm you understand. For example, if Cindy says, "The party will be at my house next weekend," you might respond with, "Next weekend at your place sounds great!"

Avoiding Common Pitfalls: Being interrupted is one of the biggest turn-offs to someone who is speaking. Similarly, being distracted, like playing with your phone or multitasking while someone is speaking shows you aren't really listening. Being judgmental about what the other person has to say is another surefire way to shut them down, as is being too quiet or forgetting what they were talking about. If you can avoid these common active listening pitfalls, you can expect to have a positive experience.

Need a little more inspiration? Here are a few exercises that can help you enhance your listening skills:

Practice Paraphrasing: Take a sentence of dialogue from a book and paraphrase it. Alternatively, ask a friend or family member about a topic you know they are interested in. Paraphrase back to them what they tell you.

Be Empathetic: Start a conversation with someone who holds a different viewpoint than you on a particular topic. Don't try to convince them to agree with your view, simply listen and try to focus on the reasoning behind their beliefs.

Eliminate Distractions: Bye bye cell phone! Many of us tend to use our cell phone as a crutch in social situations. During your next conversation, make a conscious effort to avoid checking your phone or looking around at other people or things.

THE ART OF ASKING QUESTIONS

Asking questions is a great tool for keeping conversations flowing. However, asking the right questions is an artform all in itself. Children are naturals when it comes to asking questions, even if they don't have a filter most of the time ("Mommy, why doesn't that man have any hair?"). As adults, we lose the ability to ask questions for one reason or another; maybe we don't want to sound silly or stupid, or maybe we don't want to be a bother. But in conversation, asking questions can be an effective way to show interest and encourage the other party to open up.

Different questions have different effects, so being mindful of what, how and when you ask is important. Knowing the difference between open-ended questions and closed questions can help you steer the conversation in the direction you want it to go. When you're trying to strike up a conversation and get to know someone better, open-ended questions are generally regarded as the better choice. They usually lead to more discovery, and allow the person you're speaking with to express their feelings and opinions in their own way.

Open-ended questions guide the other person to give their opinion or offer more details. These types of questions are ideal for when you want feedback or want to continue the conversation. Open-ended questions usually start with who, what, when, where, why, or how, and encourage a full answer. For example, "What made you decide to go to Ireland for vacation?" is an open-ended question that could lead to even more interesting conversation!

Closed questions typically come with a predefined set of one word answers, like "yes" or "no." If you can sense that it's time to end the conversation, a closed question is best for keeping things short. For example, "Did you go to Ireland for your vacation?" is an example of a closed question. The interaction can reasonably end here and still be polite, but if either of you wish, additional follow-up questions can be asked to keep the conversation flowing.

It's also important to avoid asking intrusive questions, like inquiring about personal information. If you are speaking with someone who has an ill family member, it might not be appropriate to ask what their specific illness is. Instead, you might ask a general question, like "How is [name of family member] doing?" and let the other person open up to you as much as they feel comfortable doing.

Practice Questions to Try: The next time you find yourself in a social situation or having a conversation with someone new, consider asking them an open-ended question. Use active listening to decide which part of the conversation to inquire about, and be ready to ask a sincere question. Start your sentence with one of these examples and tailor the rest of your question to the specific topic.

"Who did you xxx?"
"What do you think of xxx?"
"When did you xxx?"
"Where did you hear about xxx?"
"Why do you think xxx?"
"How did you xxx?"

You've now mastered the art of asking questions!

CREATING EMOTIONAL CONNECTIONS

When we first encounter a new person, we are strangers. All we know about the other person is what we have detected from their appearance, their body language, and the way they interact with their surroundings. It may seem like making an emotional connection with a perfect stranger is impossible, but it's actually easier than you think. After all, we're all human and have similar wants and needs, right? The key to creating a deep emotional connection during conversations is by displaying empathy.

Empathy makes having a conversation that goes back and forth like ping pong a breeze. When we show empathy, it helps the individual we are speaking with feel that we actually care about not just what they have to say, but about them as a person. When we are empathetic, we can better relate to others, making conversation more natural and pleasant. Many of the most successful leaders in the world have a high "EQ," or emotional intelligence, and place empathy high on their list of business priorities for this very reason.

> "Being a good listener, finding empathy, understanding emotions, communicating effectively, treating people well, and bringing out the best is critical to success. It will also help you build a business that really understands people and solves their problems, and it will make for a happier and healthier team too."
>
> — RICHARD BRANSON

A no-fail way to express your empathetic feelings in conversation is by responding to their words in a kind and supportive way. Let's go back to the person with an ill family member. As they open up to you and describe their hardships or feelings in dealing with the situation, you may naturally find yourself adapting your facial features and body language in response. Match your words to your expressions, with phrases like "I'm sorry to hear that" or "I can only imagine how hard that must be."

Navigating sensitive topics like these can be tricky, but simply letting the person talk and using active listening will take you far. Avoid starting with your own thoughts or telling a story of a similar experience that you or someone else had. You can utilize asking questions within reason, as long as you keep them respectful and unintrusive. If you are worried for the person, feel free to express your concern without criticizing them, and offer help if you are able or willing.

Another way to connect on a deeper level is by building trust through vulnerability. In romantic relationships, for example, being vulnerable is a way to show the other person that you care. When we are vulnerable, we open ourselves up to being potentially hurt or criticized. Some of our secrets may be told, or information that isn't public or readily available may be shared. Depending on the situation, you can build trust with someone through simple admissions of what makes you vulnerable. For example, if you are speaking to someone about her party, you could share that you admire her party-planning skills, and admit that you wished you were as organized as she. As always, when you are speaking with someone new, avoid TMI (Too Much Information!) when it comes to your weaknesses, fears or secrets. Sharing too much will only scare a new friend away!

Upgrade your emotional IQ: Put yourself in someone else's shoes for an afternoon. Learn something that you didn't know before about new people in your life. Focus on what makes you similar to them, rather than different. If possible, seek these people out and listen to what they have to say.

Bonus: Connect with a social action movement or non-profit organization and volunteer!

MAINTAINING CONVERSATIONAL FLOW

So you've nailed your introduction, the ice is broken, and you've told a story that has their attention. Now it's up to you to keep that conversation flowing. Depending on the circumstance and situation, your conversation may be brief, and that's okay. But if you really want to get to know someone or foster a connection, then maintaining a rapport is what you should aim for.

No conversation is without speed bumps, but there are a few ways you can ensure smooth sailing when chatting with a new friend or acquaintance.

Avoid Awkward Silences: Are those crickets? Sometimes, no matter how hard you try to engage or ask questions, a conversation just stalls. Maybe you were interrupted by an outside source or maybe you just drew a blank. Here's how to steer the conversation back around and get talking again.

- *Read the situation:* Is the person you're speaking to uncomfortable? Maybe they have to use the bathroom or they're running late! Don't ruin your chance to connect with them again. Check in and see if they're okay or if they need to go somewhere. If not, proceed to the next step.
- *Ask for stories:* Just like with asking open-ended questions, stories can lead to discovery and the creation of a genuine bond. Don't ask for definite, one-word answers. That will bring your conversation to a halt.
- *Don't say everything all at once:* As with creating suspense, treat your words like breadcrumbs or precious stones. Disperse your storytelling tidbits one at a time and you'll be less likely to have dead air between you and your conversational companion.

Gracefully Change the Subject: It happens; sometimes, we just pick a bad topic to discuss. Time to change the subject! This is where you break out your "Uno Reverse" card and make lemonade out of those lemons. Use the current subject matter that isn't working as a "reminder" jumping off point to introduce a new topic. You might say something like, "I'm glad you brought that up, that reminds me…" and then, ta-da! You're onto a new topic. Easy!

Another thing to remember when managing the flow of your conversation is to make sure to balance speaking and listening. As we've gone over before, no one likes a person who only talks about themself. Think of your conversation as a game (ping pong, remember?). You serve up, then they serve back. If you find yourself taking over the conversation, take a step back and ask an open-ended question. Similarly, if you feel like you aren't contributing enough, launch into a story or interject with nods, body language and affirmative phrases like "Yes, I agree" or "I see" to show you're still engaged.

Keep your conversation exciting!

- Have an intention for the conversation
- Smile
- Make eye contact
- Practice active listening
- Ask interesting questions
- Avoid controversial topics
- Seek out mutual interests

Practice Time: Ask a mutual friend or relative to engage in a mock discussion with you and have them purposely throw in some conversational road blocks. Ask them to randomly create an awkward silence and practice turning the conversation back around. Have them bring up a surprising uncomfortable topic and find a way to use it to change the subject. Remember, practice makes perfect, so don't be afraid to have multiple mock conversations.

YOUR MISSION

Start a captivating conversation. The next time you find yourself in a social situation, whether you're waiting in line at the coffee shop or volunteering at a non-profit, chat up a new person. Use the skills outlined in this chapter to create an emotional connection with empathy, ask questions and try your hand at becoming a storytelling pro. After your encounter, evaluate how it went, what you could have done differently, what went wrong, and more importantly, what went right. Pat yourself on the back for being brave!

3

MASTERING BODY LANGUAGE

Before you speak a single word, your body language has already said a great deal. Mastering the language of your body can unlock the secret to successful and influential communication and help you impart the right message. How you carry yourself shows a lot about how you feel about yourself, and can subconsciously tell potential conversational partners how you feel about yourself, too.

Consider how you might view another person based on their body language alone. Are their shoulders slouched? Are their hands balled into fists? Are they leaning back in their seat? What do you think these body positions mean? The fact is, body language signals can have very different meanings across cultures, genders and in different social situations. A gesture that may be harmless in one culture could be very offensive in another.

So how can we be sure what people's body language means? The truth is, we can't. It used to be commonly thought that crossing your legs toward someone meant that you're engaged in the conversation (and also might be an invitation for romance). The truth might simply be that you were uncomfortable with the way you were sitting and had to shift your position! Misinterpreting someone's body language can be embarrassing, and getting it right 100% of the time isn't a reality. Psychology expert Vincent Denault explains that there isn't a universal body language.

> *"When specific gestures are associated with specific meanings, and when this is implicitly or explicitly presented as scientific, then it begins to fall under the umbrella of pseudoscience,"*
>
> — VINCENT DENAULT

Educating yourself about the most common types of body language, cultural differences, and common misunderstandings in non-verbal communication is a great first step in becoming a body language master. You won't get it right every time, but when you pair body language with a person's words and use other contextual clues, you'll often be able to decode what they're trying to say.

Read on for all the tips and tricks you need to know to become a master body language interpreter.

DECIPHERING NON-VERBAL CUES

The words we say don't always match up with what we mean or are feeling. Consider your own experiences in social situations; have you ever lied and said, "I'm fine!" when you were actually uncomfortable? Many of us were taught to "grin and bear it," so there may be pain behind our smiles. Understanding the subtleties of facial expressions, gestures, and posture can help you determine if your conversational partner really means what they are saying.

The art of body language is called Kinesics, a term coined by Dr. Albert Mehrabian. In Kinesics we learn what the following facial expressions typically mean:

Laughing: Happiness, humor, enjoyment
Crying: Sadness, distress, pain
Smiling: Friendliness, happiness, positive emotions
Frowning: Sadness, negative emotions, disapproval
Winking: Flirtation, playfulness, sexual attraction, humor
Scowling: Frustration, disapproval, anger
Raised Eyebrows: Surprise, approval, confusion, skepticism
Furrowed Brows: Frustration, anger, concentration

Gestures are another way we nonverbally express ourselves, often without even realizing it. The two types of gestures commonly displayed are illustrative and affective. We use illustrative gestures to reinforce the meaning of our words, for example hand motions, pointing or mimicking. Active gestures involve the facial expressions mentioned above that help to further express our emotions when we cannot find the words.

Posture is also important in understanding how someone is feeling. As we have mentioned before, paying attention to whether or not someone is making eye contact, has their arms crossed, or is leaning in toward you will tell you a lot about their true emotional state. By understanding these cues and acting accordingly during conversation, you can help strengthen bonds with new friends and acquaintances.

When you're speaking with someone from a different cultural background than you, language barriers might not be the only thing standing in your way. Let's take a few unique body language gestures from around the world and talk about what they mean. For example, in the film *Inglourious Basterds,* the faux German spy gives himself away when he uses the American hand signal for the number three. There are many unique cultural body language gestures to know, but here are some of the most common you may encounter.

Germany: Counting begins with the thumb, not the pointer finger as it does in the US.
India: Nodding the head in agreement is expressed from left to right, instead of up and down.
Italy: Hands in the "pinecone," or palms up and fingers pointed position indicates exasperation.
Japan: Direct eye contact can signal disrespect and aggression.
Switzerland: A three-cheek kiss starting on the right is a common greeting.
Korea: Bowing is a greeting; how low you go indicates your level of respect.
Russia: Counting on the fingers begins with an open palm as a countdown, ending in a fist.
Iran: In many Middle Eastern cultures, thumbs up is the equivalent of giving the middle finger!
China: Pointing to the nose instead of the chest indicates pride of self.
France: Palm pointed down and rocking side to side is used for the expression "so-so."

PROJECTING CONFIDENCE THROUGH POSTURE

There's a reason your parents and teachers told you not to slouch! Not only is it better for your posture, but standing up straight helps with your confidence, too. Having good posture is a nonverbal cue that lets people know we are confident and sincere, which will make us seem more approachable to prospective new friends.

Creating a commanding and powerful presence is easier than you think. Here are a few posture tips to help you strike a powerful pose wherever your feet take you.

Stand Up Straight: Spine erect, shoulders back, chest out.
Asymmetrical Stance: Take up some space without encroaching on others to command a presence.
Walk with a Purpose: Whether you're heading to the gym, to catch the bus or just around the block, walk like you have a purpose in mind.
Pretend You're a Superhero: We all know superheroes never slouch!
Chin Up: Just like standing up straight, remembering to keep your chin up helps you appear more confident.
Hands Out of Pockets: Hiding your hands in your pockets is a sign of insecurity. Set those fingers free!

Posture impacts not only the way others perceive you but how you perceive yourself. If you are tired, you may find yourself slouching, and then feeling like you are less confident. A person with poor body posture indicates disinterest or uncertainty, which is something we don't want to project to anyone, especially new connections.

If you often fall into bad posture without realizing it, the good news is that you can train yourself. Here are a few exercises to help you have better posture and improve your overall body language.

Be Aware: Just being mindful of your posture is the first step. Practice consistently remembering to straighten up, even when you're doing chores or hanging out at home. This will do wonders for your posture.

Get an Ergonomic Desk Setup: As I'm writing this, I'm subconsciously planting my feet on the floor, straightening my spine and lifting my chin! Make some adjustments at your workspace or computer desk to ensure you don't slouch.

Exercise: Not only will it make you feel better and improve your overall health, getting fit will help with your posture, too. You might even consider working with a professional trainer to safely help tone posture-related muscles.

Stretch: As with exercise, gentle stretching can help you move and bend and achieve better overall posture. Try some light yoga or stretching and see if your posture improves.

Choose Supportive Footwear: High heels are cute, but they can affect the body's center of gravity. When standing for long periods of time, choose shoes with good support.

Some people simply command presence, and unless you've studied body language, it may be hard to understand why. These individuals know how to light up a room, draw everyone's gaze and keep the interest of everyone around them. Read on and see if you agree.

PUBLIC FIGURES WITH COMMANDING PRESENCE

Marilyn Monroe: A cultural icon of beauty and sexuality, Marilyn was more than just a pretty face. The combination of her striking appearance and signature confidence has become known as the "Marilyn Effect," and her methods are still mimicked by celebrities today.

Denzel Washington: Known for his engaging and powerful performances, Denzel oozes confidence in the way he holds himself and speaks. He delivers his lines with a measure of calm, and as a result, viewers perceive him as being intense and having a sense of authority.

Franklin Delano Roosevelt: FDR created a powerful bond with the American people by communicating with them in a way no other president had before, with his "fireside chats." These intimate exchanges paired with his stoic nature helped him gain his constituents' trust.

Oprah Winfrey: The talk show host gained world-wide fame for her ability to connect with guests and her audience on a deep, emotional level. When she sits with her guests, her posture is relaxed and opened, which encourages them to trust her and open up.

Think about orators, teachers, or figures in your day-to-day life who have caught your attention. Think about the people you respect and look up to, how they carry themselves and the way they speak. What can you glean from their outward appearance and behaviors to help you feel more confident in speaking to others?

THE POWER OF FACIAL EXPRESSIONS

Being aware of your facial expressions is one of the most important things we can do as communicators. Ideally, the person you are speaking with will be reading your expression as you talk and engaging in direct eye contact with you. Controlling and utilizing your facial expressions effectively can be the difference between making a good or bad impression.

You may have heard of the very southern expression, "Fix your face." If you're like me, it's hard not to wear your heart on your sleeve. When I was younger, if I was pleased with a situation (or more likely than not, displeased) the furrows in my brow and my downturned lips usually gave away how I felt. While in most cases we shouldn't suppress the way we feel, there are some situations when you will definitely need to learn to control your facial expressions. For example, if you have a job interview, but you are nervous, learning to control your facial expressions will make you seem more confident. If you are feeling unwell, controlling your facial expressions may be impossible, so consider whether or not you need to sit out a social situation until you're feeling more up to the task.

Controlling Your Facial Expression:

Don't Forget to Smile: If you aren't someone who naturally smiles when you meet new people, practice smiling in the privacy of your own home. Smile at your pet, your television, your mirror, wherever! Make smiling your default when you want to appear more approachable.

Keep it Neutral: Practice a neutral facial expression, as well. You don't have to smile at everyone you see, but you shouldn't frown either. Your facial expression should be relaxed, neither happy nor sad, with your facial muscles relaxed.

So Serious: Show you are paying attention in a serious situation. Keep direct eye contact, knit your brow and show concern without scowling or frowning.

Get Feedback: Practice your facial expressions and get feedback from a friend or relative. Does your happy expression look too happy? Does your serious expression make you look angry? Is your neutral expression as good as it can be? Feedback helps you see your blind spots and the areas you need to work on.

Our expressions can be infectious, so putting out the type of expression we want to see in others begins with us. Smiling has been shown to help reduce stress hormones in the bloodstream and enhance positive emotions. Smiling and laughing naturally helps us to tap into our positive emotions, and helps others to view us in a positive light. Frowns naturally have the opposite effect, and can make you seem less approachable.

Micro-expressions are little facial expressions that we may not realize we are making but which can still make a big impact. For example, flared nostrils might make someone think that you disapprove or are aggressive (think about a bull with its flared nostrils!). According to the FBI, there are seven universal facial expressions (cite); Happiness, Surprise, Contempt, Sadness, Fear, Disgust and Anger. The FBI can use their knowledge of micro-expressions to tell whether a suspect is sad or filled with contempt. For example, the mouth may turn down and eyes may be soft when someone is sad. However, if their nostrils are also flared, or their lips are curled, a person may feel contempt. Being able to tell the difference between micro expressions can be a big indicator in how someone really is feeling.

Remember: If your goal is to make new friends or business connections, then maintaining an approachable, engaging demeanor is key. Be sure to choose a moment when you are feeling and looking your best to ensure your expression matches your inner feelings. Practice "fixing your face" when dealing with situations where your facial expressions may betray you. Most of all, don't forget to smile!

GESTURES THAT ENHANCE COMMUNICATION

Have you ever met an enthusiastic person who likes to talk with their hands? Former German Chancellor Angela Merkel was so well known for her infamous diamond-shaped hand gesture that it was even coined the Merkel-Raute, or Merkel Rhombus. It is said that the former chancellor adopted this stance as a way to find something neutral to do with her hands when she was speaking.

Avoiding unusual hand gestures is a smart move for everyone, and not just politicians! Certain hand gestures, such as the one that Americans use for "OK," are offensive in other cultures, or could have a nefarious meaning. Hand gestures can also be distracting when you are trying to speak. Wild or overly dramatic gestures can detract from the message you are trying to impart rather than enhance it. Keep emphatic gestures, such as pointing, showing how wide or tall something is, clapping, fist pumps and others to a minimum if you want to have the greatest impact.

If you find that you simply can't control your hand movements, don't fall back on hiding them in your pocket. Instead, be like Angela Merkel and find a comfortable way to hold your hands during conversation, such as folded across your lap. If you do use your hands, try to gesture symmetrically, with both hands moving in tandem with one another. Otherwise, keep those hands comfortably at your sides until you feel compelled to gesture again.

MIRRORING FOR RAPPORT BUILDING

Mirror, mirror, on the wall, who's the most approachable of all? It's you! Or rather, it will be if you learn the technique of mirroring. I'm not suggesting that you become a copycat of the person you're speaking to, but much like reading the room, reading someone's body language and "mirroring" it shows that you are paying attention to their micro-facial expressions and cues.

Mirroring is a behavior in which one person subconsciously imitates a speech pattern, attitude or gesture of another person. This often happens in social situations among friends or families and often goes unnoticed . Mirroring can be used to help establish and display empathy and understanding with new people, and can be as simple as displaying the same expression or body language as them.

One thing to be careful of, though, in mirroring, is that it not come across as mocking the other person. The person you are speaking with may have a different accent than you or a different cadence of speech. You must take care not to copy them directly to avoid insulting or embarrassing them.

Successful Examples of Mirroring

Your friend is telling you about the new job she was just hired for. She is excited, her eyes are wide and there is a big smile on her face. Her voice is high and her hands are animated as she tells you about her new job. This is an excellent opportunity to mirror her enthusiasm by matching her smile, nodding, and adding excitement and enthusiasm to your own voice.

Perhaps another new acquaintance is telling you about the death of his uncle. His brow may be furrowed, his mouth turned down and his hands folded in his lap. Consider matching his facial expressions in a less intense way, by knitting your own brows, keeping your lips in a neutral position, and your hands in your lap. Nod and use active listening to show you're engaged in the conversation and are empathetic.

At the end of the day, mirroring is all about "matching the other person's energy" in a way that is authentic and effective.

YOUR MISSION

This week, make a plan to improve your body posture. Update your workspace, if needed, to make it more ergonomic, start a fitness or stretching routine to improve your physical state and be mindful of your posture wherever you go.

Bonus: Have a conversation with someone and make a mental note of your gestures and facial expressions. What are your crutches or most used expressions?

4

RAPID RAPPORT-BUILDING TECHNIQUES

"What greater thing is there for two human souls than to feel that they are joined for life ... to strengthen each other ... to be at one with each other in silent, unspeakable memories."

— GEORGE ELIOT, ENGLISH NOVELIST AND POET

Have you ever met someone in line at a theme park or on a plane and in a matter of minutes felt as though this person could be your best friend? Have you met someone who could seamlessly carry on a conversation on anything from the weather to what kind of shirt you're wearing, and then all of a sudden you're chatting about your favorite movies and music? It's likely that you encountered a master of rapport.

Imagine being able to create a bond almost instantly with someone you just met. What kind of doors could that intimate connection open up? What kind of new opportunities could be offered to you if you could be seen as a confidante from the get-go? This chapter is designed to help you unlock the techniques rapport masters use to turn fleeting interactions into an ongoing discussion with just about anyone.

THE FUNDAMENTALS OF RAPPORT

Rapport refers to a close and harmonious relationship in which the people or groups concerned are "in sync" with one another, understand one another's feelings or ideas, and communicate effortlessly. Think of rapport as a conversational game of tennis or ping pong, where the excitement of the words and ideas flow in a continual, steady-paced back and forth. When you have rapport with someone, you are able to match their energy, be enthusiastic about sharing ideas, and speak and talk to each other in equal measure.

Synching up with your conversational partners is an important aspect of building a relationship with someone. Think about your friend base, chosen family, or the people in your circle; they are the ones you lean on and have a lasting relationship with. These people may be easier for you to talk to, and probably share the same values and interests as you. If you can't keep the conversation flowing or find any common ground, then any hope of fostering a long-lasting relationship could be dead in the water.

The first stage of rapport-building is coordination. This is where body language mirroring comes into play. Be sure to match the person's emotional state, their posture, and the speed and volume of their voice in order to keep them engaged. The second stage is showing mutual attentiveness, meaning reciprocating nonverbal cues like nodding. This acknowledges that you're being attentive to their needs. Finally, practice commonality, where you intentionally try to find something you have in common with the person you're speaking with, whether that's an interest in sports, your home life or something else. Sharing personal details about yourself (only to the level you're comfortable with) is a great way to quickly build rapport with anyone.

Building rapport is important in a number of professional and interpersonal relationships, particularly those that require a level of trust. Consider the trust that patients put in their healthcare providers; when a person's health or life is on the line, bedside manner is an important part of providing care. When a patient feels at ease with their doctor, dentist, or therapist, they'll be more likely to relax and will be more receptive to care.

Building rapport is also essential for those in sales, as "America's Greatest Salesman," Ben Feldman discovered. In post-WW II America, Feldman was a high-school dropout who went on to have a 50-year career, writing over $1.5 billion in life insurance policies. Feldman spent his lifetime building a rapport with clients and colleagues, and by his 80s, when he became ill, his influence had such a far reach that his supporters came out in droves. In 1992, after suffering a cerebral oedema, his employer, New York Life, created a sales competition in his honor. Feldman went on to win that competition from his hospital bed, selling $15 million in life insurance policies, thanks to his rapport-building skills.

How can you tell if your rapport-building is effective? Are you coming on too strong, or engaging just right? Grab a friend, start a conversation and give these self-assessment exercises a try!

Practice Making a Good Introduction: Break out that handshake and eye contact!
Lead with Empathy: Are you coming off snarky or uninterested? Be empathetic.
Practice Active Listening: Remember to be authentic and attentive.
Find Commonalities: What do you and your conversational partner have in common?

Ask Engaging Questions: Are you talking about yourself too much?

Be Aware of Body Language: How are you sitting or standing? What are your facial expressions like?

FINDING COMMON GROUND QUICKLY

So you only have a few minutes to catch the interest of your conversational partner. How can you get your new acquaintance to open up to you quickly and establish a rapport? Finding common ground is easier than you may think; everyone is human, after all! We have the same core needs, wants and desires. What you need to do to build rapport is discover what those commonalities are. You can do this by becoming a personal interests detective.

Sometimes you only have a few moments to evaluate the person you're conversing with. In these instances, it's important to think fast on your feet and use all of your senses and conversational skills to decide what to say. Here are a few tips for discovering shared interests, so you can get the ball rolling.

Look for Non-Verbal Clues: Are they wearing a shirt with a sports team or a band label? Do they have tattoos? Pet hair on their shirt? Are they wearing a wedding ring, or speak with a distinctive regional accent? Use these non-verbal clues for the next step!

Ask Questions: Once you've discovered something distinct about the person you're speaking with, ask a question about it. Just make sure your questions aren't too personal or inappropriate so you don't come across as rude or intrusive.

Talk about Your Interests: If all else fails, organically bring up a hobby, television show or sport you enjoy. If you talk about, for instance, the martial arts class you attend, you may discover that the person you're speaking with is into another sport. You can then pivot the conversation away from martial arts and talk about their sport instead.

One of the more difficult aspects of finding common ground is being able to adapt to different personality types. An extrovert may have a hard time getting an introvert to open up, for example. Being able to change your approach when someone is more reserved is essential for keeping conversational pathways open. This is where you need to use all your tools to read the body language and other non-verbal cues of your conversational partner. Shifting gears when you come in contact with different personality types is easier when you utilize mirroring tactics to "match" their energy.

But what happens when you're having a conversation amongst a diverse group and the topic goes off course in a bad way? The knee-jerk reaction might be to change the subject, but that could leave certain members of the group feeling alienated or hurt. It's always important to be inclusive, especially in diverse settings, and make sure everyone feels heard and that their ideas and opinions are valued. Below are some ways to take the reins and be sure the conversation goes smoothly.

Ask for Permission: Just because you know that someone may be disabled, BIPOC (black, indigenous or other people of color) or LGBTQ+ doesn't mean they want to discuss their disability, culture or identity. Give them an opportunity to accept or decline discussing sensitive matters.

Create a Comfortable Atmosphere: Is everyone comfortable? Are there refreshments? Is the setting a calm one? Consider what you can do to manipulate the environment and make everyone involved feel more at ease.

Listen: Give them the floor! When dealing with issues that don't pertain to you, or are not your lived experience or specialty, listen more than you speak. You'll find it's easier to gain trust from those who may be reserved if you offer an empathetic ear and allow them to be heard.

Another way to develop an instant sense of rapport is by remembering personal details. Remembering someone's name is a powerful way to show them that you really care about them and remember them. One of my favorite instances of this is in the movie *House Bunny*, starring Anna Farris. In this film, Farris is entering a new sorority house and wants to remember everyone's name, so she repeats their name back in a silly voice. She uses the classic tip of saying and repeating someone's name out loud to remember!

We won't be instant best friends with everyone we meet, and that's not the goal here. However, finding common ground is a great way to learn about your neighbors, your co-workers and new acquaintances.

THE ROLE OF EMPATHY AND VALIDATION

Merriam-Webster defines empathy as "the action of understanding, being aware of, being sensitive to, and vicariously experiencing the feelings, thoughts, and experience of another."

Let's be real; it isn't always easy to be empathetic toward someone who has drastically different values and beliefs from your own, especially if you perceive those beliefs to be harmful. The old saying to "walk a mile in someone else's shoes" is about handling this very situation. People come to conclusions or hold beliefs because their life experience has guided them to think and feel that way. In order to be a truly empathetic listener, it's your job to see the whole picture and try to understand what they've been through.

One of the ways you can show empathy is by validating the feelings of others. Validating others' feelings and perspectives is essential to building rapport, and can build emotional bridges that were not there before. One of the best ways to do this is to incorporate validating statements into your conversation. You can utilize phrases like:

"What a frustrating situation."
"I can understand why you feel that way."
"I know this is very important to you."
"I see that this is upsetting to you."
"Let me see if I am understanding this correctly…"

The real key to using validating statements is to empathize without sounding insincere or patronizing. Emotions can run high if the topic of discussion becomes too personal, or if you forget your role as an empathetic listener. Being condescending, insulting, or speaking in a manner that feels patronizing will only shut the other person down. Emotional invalidation leads the other person to feel judged, rejected or ignored, something you certainly don't want when trying to build a rapport. The bottom line: show you are listening, even if you disagree.

Words are important, but they aren't the only tools we have when it comes to communicating with others. Practicing validation and using your non-verbal skills can really help break down walls. Here are a few ways to put this practice into action:

Be Aware of Your Physical Gestures: Remember to fix your face! Keep your expressions neutral to avoid sending mixed messages, and be sure to use similarly neutral or positive body language. Make appropriate eye contact, and match the other person's energy.

Practice Mindful Listening: Really pay attention to what the person is saying, and avoid distractions, especially your own emotions. Put away your phone, take your hands out of your pockets and listen without judging.

Validate with Mutual Attentiveness: With a blend of physical gestures and active listening, you can reciprocate by sharing personal details about yourself. This will signal to the other person that you are being attentive to their needs and being vulnerable with them, too.

ADJUSTING COMMUNICATION STYLE

In professional situations, it's often necessary to learn how to adjust your communication style to fit your colleagues and co-workers. In small and large business settings alike, emotions can run high and miscommunications can create professional rifts that are hard to overcome. Consider this real-life situation from a woman we'll call "Molly":

"Recently, I was hired to replace a much-beloved member of my company after he'd retired," Molly said. "There was one man at the company who didn't seem to warm up to me. I am a naturally outgoing person, but my male co-worker was very reserved and direct. It took some time, but I was eventually able to maintain my personality and keep a professional relationship with him by matching his energy and keeping our interactions brief."

The situation Molly experienced with her co-worker wasn't all that uncommon. In work environments, schools and other social situations, we are often tasked with sharing space with people who are very different from us. Molly was able to overcome this situation by doing the following:

Identify: Discover what the root of your communication issue is. What is this person's preferred communication style? Are they reserved? Stand-offish? Are they on the spectrum? Consider everything you can learn about your acquaintance to tailor your conversations.

Adapt: Try different approaches with the people you are attempting to speak to, and see which are the most effective. Think out of the box and get creative. Don't give up!

Often in communication, it isn't what we say, but how we say it. A simple phrase like "thanks" can be interpreted differently, depending on the way it's said. "Thanks" with a pleasant voice and an even tone is meant as a genuine sign of appreciation. "Thanks" said with a clipped, mocking tone indicates that the person means the exact opposite.

Tempo and language choices similarly help to set the tone in communication styles. Someone who speaks too fast or with too much enthusiasm may be tiring or exasperating to talk to. Likewise, if you speak in a dull, slow, monotonous voice, you may bore the person you're speaking to. You might also consider your language choices when trying to tailor your communication style. For example, expletives and slang are generally regarded as no-no's in professional conversations or when meeting someone new. Harsh language can be off-putting and make you seem like you're unpleasant to talk to.

Being an agreeable person to speak to is one thing, but you must also be able to assert yourself if a meeting or introduction becomes hostile. One thing I hope you won't do is continue a conversation that makes you uncomfortable, especially if you have tried to turn things around. We've talked a lot about how you should drive the conversation, and how it's up to you to meet the person you've approached on their level, but sometimes conversations just can't be saved. If the person you are speaking with becomes angry or annoyed, it is always best to politely bow out.

you still find yourself struggling with the notion of adapting to different behaviors, remember you can always practice at home first. One of the easiest ways to do this is to watch TV! Choose one of your favorite sitcoms, preferably one with a diverse cast, and watch as the characters interact with one another. Sitcoms offer classic examples of people with different personalities clashing in humorous ways. Feel free to take notes when there are conflicts or miscommunications, then figure out what you might have said or done differently in those situations. Often, observing other people and situations and learning from their mistakes is a effective way to avoid making those mistakes yourself.

DEEPENING CONNECTIONS

Beginning a conversation with musings about how pleasant the weather is or how delicious the eggplant parmigiana is are fine when meeting someone new. But those surface-level topics don't often lead to deeper conversation and deeper connections. If you're looking to truly connect with someone, then relating to them on a deeper level is essential. If your conversation is going well, and you want to dig deeper and truly connect with someone, here are some excellent techniques for encouraging them to open up:

Ask Thoughtful Questions: Don't be afraid to ask them about their feelings and experiences. Encourage them to tell you what's really in their hearts and on their minds about topics like current events, music, art, film or sports. Ask about the things that they like, their preferences and interests.

Be Patient: Give your conversational partner some space, and wait for them to respond to your queries. Don't push and don't change the topic right away! Sometimes folks are shy about revealing things about themselves, but you can help keep the door open by being patient and waiting.

Be Attentive: Listen and respond in kind when they share their innermost thoughts and feelings. Reciprocate with your own experiences and thoughts and find out if you share similar ideas and values.

> *"On sensitive issues, talk isn't cheap — it takes real courage to pry open topics nailed shut."*
>
> — MARVIN OLASKY, PROFESSOR AND AUTHOR

There are times when a new acquaintance might shy away from engaging in an open interaction. But then there are oversharers, who might bombard you with sensitive information that you were not prepared to hear. Just as with all other conversational situations, don't forget that you're in the driver's seat; it's up to you to anticipate bumps in the road before they even happen.

Be Proactive: Like a road sign that warns about slippery ice ahead, prepare yourself for icy conversational roads ahead. If you can sense that the conversation is about to veer into uncharted territory or dangerous waters, try to navigate the conversation in a new direction. The best bet is always to shut down uncomfortable topics before they even come up.

Be Empathetic: If someone divulged something very personal to you, and it makes you uncomfortable to continue talking about it, you don't have to indulge them. Simply offer a neutral facial expression paired with a similarly neutral expression like "I'm sorry to hear that" or "That sounds like quite an experience."

Turn it Around: If your conversation partner continues to make you uncomfortable, change the subject or bow out of the conversation. If you remain in, depending on the level of sensitivity, you can use the topic as a jumping-off point to bring up a new subject.

Self-disclosure plays a major role when it comes to deepening connections. When you share your own experiences, it helps to validate the feelings of the person you're speaking with. If you share something low-risk and personal about yourself first, for example, that you are feeling nervous at a conference, that will give your conversational partner a hint that you are feeling a little vulnerable, too.

Research shows self-disclosure can play a major role when it comes to forming deep relationships. Self-disclosure can bring people closer, help them better understand each other, and cooperate better. Particularly important are emotional disclosures, because they help boost empathy and build trust.

Dealing with uncomfortable conversations isn't easy, but once again, you can practice at home. Let's turn again to the TV for an at-home taste of real-world conflicts. Choose your favorite drama or soap opera, one with a variety of cast members, and watch as difficult conversations play out. See how the characters react to one another and take note of what works and what doesn't.

YOUR MISSION

Make a deeper connection. This week I want you to identify someone you've been able to start a conversation with whom you would like to know better. Use the tools in this chapter to approach them and build a better rapport. Open up and disclose something personal about yourself, all while using active listening and empathy. See if you can meet them on their level, match their energy and forge a deeper level of communication with your new colleague or friend!

5

WORKING A ROOM LIKE A PRO

"This is my one chance to make a great entrance! My whole life, I have never made a great entrance!"

— GEORGE COSTANZA, SEINFELD

The world is a movie, and you're the main character — step into every room like you're ready to steal the show! A room full of strangers can be your greatest opportunity if you know the art of making each moment count. This chapter is designed to help you work the room like a pro. Whether you'd like to enhance your image in the business world, or are simply interested in making more friends, it's important to think of every social interaction as a possibility for networking. From baby showers to conventions and beyond, we'll show you how to seize the opportunity to make the most out of any event.

PREPARATION AND MINDSET

As a former scout, I know all too well the motto "Be Prepared." While you won't be starting campfires or dressing wounds during your social interactions (hopefully!) this is a helpful motto for anyone when meeting new people. Getting yourself into the preparedness mindset will set you up for success and help you to be more comfortable and natural in the way you speak and present yourself. Below are a few techniques for researching and preparing to speak to others at various events.

Research the Location: **Pull up your internet browser and research the restaurant, convention center, or outdoor space of whatever event you will be attending. Where are the bathrooms? Where will the food and drinks be served? Where will your seat be located? Who will you be seated next to?**

Research the Attendees: **Look** up some of the people who will be attending the same event as you (not in a creepy way!). If you're going to a business convention, find out who the key speakers will be and learn about their platforms. If you are going to your cousin's wedding, find out which of their friends will be in attendance so you can think ahead about ways to connect with them. If you are going to a convention, research some topics relevant to the convention that you might raise when you meet someone new.

Be Comfortable and Relaxed: This is a useful rule that applies to all interactions. Research the event and make sure you are dressed accordingly. Remember what happened to Bridget in the movie *Bridget Jones's Diary* when she didn't read the dress code for the Tarts and Vicars luncheon? Don't start out embarrassing yourself by wearing the wrong thing! Also be sure to check the weather and make sure you have a coat or umbrella if you need it.

One of my biggest blocks when it comes to speaking with anyone new is my social anxiety (you'll notice I'm opening up with you to establish trust and empathy). I've suffered with social and generalized anxiety my entire life, and speaking to anyone new used to absolutely terrify me. I still find myself overwhelmed when speaking in front of a crowd, but I've worked hard to become comfortable speaking with people one-on-one. Here are a few tips I've found to be helpful in building my confidence and overcoming social anxiety.

Identify Triggers: What are some things that make you the most anxious? Too much noise? Don't know anyone there? Identify things that may cause you anxiety and come up with a plan to deal with them beforehand.

Control Your Breathing: Slow down! Take a breath. If I'm not being mindful, I tend to talk fast when I'm speaking. As a result, I run out of breath quickly and my anxiety peaks. Practice breathing exercises in your spare time to learn how to keep it steady and slow.

Shift Your Focus: Much of what makes us anxious is too much self-reflection. We worry about how we look or sound, or if what we are saying is wrong. Shift the focus away from yourself instead and focus on the people to whom you're speaking.

Try to Relax: What are some relaxation techniques that work for you? A calming cup of tea? Aromatherapy? Listening to music? Use whatever methods work for you before your next event or meet and greet to put yourself into a relaxed mood.

Challenge Negative Thoughts: It's easy to fall into negative thought patterns, especially about ourselves. Challenging those thoughts isn't easy, but once you stop believing the lies you tell yourself, it's easier to release the anxiety those thoughts cause. Consider the thoughts you may be having of yourself, such as "Everyone hates me" and apply them to your own thinking. Do you think that way about everyone else in the room? Of course not. So it's likely they aren't thinking about you in that way either.

Seek Professional Help: **When it comes to many of the tough subjects in this guide, remember there comes a point when we can only help ourselves so much. If you are suffering from social anxiety that is so bad it holds you back from doing the things you want to do, seek help from a professional.**

Practicing having a positive and open mindset is one of the best ways to prepare yourself for meeting someone new. If you arrive at an event or gathering already feeling anxious or negative, it will bleed into everything you do, from your body language to the tone in your voice. Finding ways to boost your confidence will go a long way toward feeling calm and confident so you can make that big entrance!

MAKING A STRONG ENTRANCE

Boxers are infamous for their ability to make an entrance. Flashing lights, an announcer gassing them up, and a powerful theme song all work together to create an intimidating presence before they even enter the ring. While you won't be able to have a pyrotechnics team or a soundboard operator to help you make a memorable entrance, you can still win over the crowd with your swagger and ensure that your next introduction is a TKO (technical knock-out).

A confident arrival can make a big impact, so knowing the right way to do it is key. Find your own hype song for yourself and follow this easy checklist to make sure your big entrance is on-point.

Be on Time: Not too early, not too late. Being on time is just right when it comes to making your entrance. While being a little early isn't bad, being late will definitely not start you off on the right foot.

Be Positive: Smile! Have we mentioned yet how important smiling is? Practice your smile for your big entrance and make sure it feels natural. Come in with a positive mood and a smile on your face to set the right tone.

Be Yourself: People are very good at picking up when someone is being false or phony. Be genuine and show off the best version of yourself to receive the best reception.

Be Appropriate: Are you wearing the right clothes? Do you have the appropriate tone of voice and body language for the situation? Be prepared and present yourself accordingly.

Be Confident: Remember how we talked about confident body language? Shoulders back, chest out, chin up, smile and offer a firm handshake when appropriate. Be open and not too rigid but stand tall!

Be Attentive: Make eye contact and engage with as many people as you can. Practice active listening as you speak to each other and build a rapport.

Now that you've made your grand entrance, it's time to read the room. When you enter a mixed group of people, not everyone is going to be receptive to your approach, even if you've made a perfect, impactful entrance. Here's a checklist you can go over to figure out whom to approach:

Read Non-Verbal Cues: Who in the group is maintaining eye contact with you? Who is returning your smile? Who looks relaxed?

Understand Nuances: Know who is in the room and how they relate to the event. Don't interrupt conversations that people are already having if they don't reciprocate your energy. Consider approaching someone who is not already engaged in a conversation.

Adjust Your Approach: Match your behavior to the tone of the room. Don't come in acting like the life of the party if the vibe is already calm and low-key.

Sometimes when you enter a room, you'll find that multiple conversations are already going on. So how do you gracefully join in? If you've already read the room, then you'll be able to tell which groups are closed off and which groups are more open to newcomers based on body language, eye contact and tone of voice. Once you've found an ongoing conversation that feels approachable, here's how you can join in:

Ask to Join: Give a general greeting and ask if you can join the conversation. Introduce yourself and make eye contact with everyone. There's always a possibility that they'll say no, so be prepared to bow out and be courteous.

Be Cool: Don't come on too strong. This may be difficult for those with animated, boisterous personalities. If you know you are a passionate, energetic person, be sure to dial it back when trying to include yourself in a new group conversating Group Dynamics

Group dynamics can be tricky to understand. Consider some infamous group dynamics from television, like on the show *Friends*. The characters in these groups have varying personalities, but were tightly knit, and there were even romantic entanglements. In *Friends*, Monica's apartment or the cafe were the usual bases where the friends met up. Her organized, assertive personality made Monica the group leader in a way. Chandler was the comedic relief, Joey was the heart-throb, Ross was the brotherly type, Rachel was the "It" girl, and Phoebe was the quirky one. Everyone had a role to play, and depending on the ebb and flow of individual relationships and romances, their roles would shift and change. Breaking into that friend group was never easy!

When I was a new hire at my corporate job many years ago, I felt like a stranger amongst a team of well-established coworkers. Everyone already seemed to know each others' personalities and had their own ongoing conversations, so breaking into their circle took time. I hung back and listened, paid attention to social cues, and eventually was invited to join in on lunches and water cooler chit chat. This work environment situation felt similar to *Friends* for me, in that I was trying to break into an established group of people who already had their own language and relationship history. I was able to keep these relationships professional while still creating an open dialogue because I waited, was patient and was able to read my new coworkers.

So, once you've got an "in" with the group you want to connect with, how do you effectively contribute to the conversation? It may seem awkward at first, as if you're barging in, but with the right knowledge, you'll be able to effortlessly interject yourself into the conversation without being awkward or uninvited. Here are some techniques to make sure you're adding something valuable to the conversation:

Share Relevant Info: Don't go off topic! Even if you're dying to add something off-topic to the conversation, don't do it. This sort of behavior often leads to hogging the conversation or taking over, which doesn't usually sit well with others.

Tell Interesting Stories: Have a backup library of stories to tell. If the conversation has gone off topic and you want to add something interesting, segue in with your own amusing anecdotes.

Don't tell tall tales, though! Be sincere, and don't be afraid to tell the story about that time a seagull stole your entire taco when you were at the beach.

Be Open: Make sure your body language remains open and approachable. Don't close yourself off from the group with non-verbal cues. Keep your expression pleasant and your body language relaxed.

Don't Hesitate: In group settings, it's even easier to become caught up worrying about making a mistake. Don't clam up and wait too long to contribute or the conversation will end before you even have a chance to speak!

Once conversations start flowing, over time, conflicts might arise. As often happens in groups, at my former job, I eventually discovered that some of my co-workers weren't so easy to get along with. It might be tempting to avoid difficult people altogether, but in some cases, it's simply not possible. Interacting with people who have challenging personalities is manageable as long as you are honest and direct. Treat them with respect and listen carefully. Focus on the facts when having a difficult conversation and avoid blaming. Most importantly, choose your words carefully and stay focused. Difficult conversations will no doubt take more work and energy, but they are important life lessons. Not everyone is going to be easy, but putting in the effort is always worth it.

CREATING A LASTING IMPACT

Merriam-Webster defines charisma as "a special magnetic charm or appeal." Some of the most famous leaders in history were able to capture the hearts and minds of a nation, for better or for worse, through their charismatic actions. Consider Nelson Mandela, Fidel Castro, Martin Luther King, Adolf Hitler and Winston Churchill, just to name a few. These leaders all were able to enthrall their followers with their charismatic personalities. Each of these leaders had memorable images, voices and powerful interactions with people, all of which worked together to create a lasting impact. Here are a few ways you can cultivate charisma and develop your own following.

Pay a Compliment: Be sincere! Keep your compliments neutral and not too personal. It can be something as simple as "I like your style!" or "I like what you did there." Giving compliments is a great way to express gratitude and give someone a boost.

Be Generous: Give your time or expertise whenever you can. Time is one of our most precious commodities, so when you help someone out, you're showing that you truly care.

Be Thankful: Say thank you often, and don't forget to say 'please' as well! Offer praise, give credit where credit is due, and show your appreciation. People tend to remember when they are made to feel appreciated.

Honor Your Word: Don't cancel meetings. Be on time. Follow through. When you keep your word, people remember you as someone who can be counted on. Being reliable is the lasting impact you want to have on others.

Be Cheerful: Smile! Laugh! Tell good-natured jokes! Not only is it more fun to converse when you're smiling and laughing, but you'll naturally release the feel-good oxytocin hormone in your brain. That's right - leaving a lasting impression is pure science!

So now that you're getting the hang of being a little more charismatic, how do you follow up and keep people engaged long after you say goodbye? When it comes to effectively maintaining connections, we need to once again look at the big picture. What will be the best way to keep in contact with the people you are engaging with? A new business partner may be more interested in connecting through a specific online social network for business, like LinkedIn, or through email. Someone you met at a party who could potentially be a new friend may want to stay in contact through social media, like Facebook or Instagram. A potential new love interest, on the other hand, may want to exchange phone numbers. Whichever way you choose to go, make sure you ask for follow-up contact information before your conversation is over, or your goodbye may be forever.

Remember, in the end, what we say and do matters, but that's not all that's at play. Leaving a lasting impression has more to do with how we make people feel. Poet and author Maya Angelou said "...people will forget what you did, but people will never forget how you made them feel." If you always make the people you're speaking with feel special, engaged, respected, and listened to, then that's the best kind of lasting impression anyone can ask for.

Practice Exchanging Info: If you feel uncomfortable asking a stranger for their contact info, a little bit of practice might help. Ask a friend or relative to help you practice different scenarios and how you can work your way into a conversation.

EVENT NETWORKING STRATEGIES

Events are some of your best opportunities to network with a wide range of people who might otherwise not be in your circle. Whether you're going to a food truck festival, superhero convention, concert or neighborhood street market, you can always find an opportunity to leverage the event. But having your strategy ready and in place beforehand is where you need to start.

Take care to balance your professional networking with socializing, particularly at events like funerals or in other sensitive situations. Part of learning to "read the room" is knowing when the right time is to bring up a topic. For example, speaking to the bride about a business proposition during her wedding reception might be a terrible idea, unless of course you and the bride already have a longstanding working rapport.

Sometimes at events like these, simply getting yourself in front of the right people is half the battle. In the comedy A *Night at the Roxbury*, the Butabi brothers wanted to meet the club owner. But no matter how hard the Butabi brothers tried, they couldn't get into the club to see him! However, after being rear-ended by a celebrity, they used their influence to get into the club and made fast friends with the owner. While that was a silly and highly unlikely scenario, it's a good example of how to seize an opportunity when it presents itself. In the real world, be sure not to use people as stepping stones, but don't be afraid to ask friends to introduce you to influential people and to help you get your foot in the proverbial door.

Here are some other ways you can seamlessly and organically widen your circle and connect with influential people.

Join Industry Groups: Is there a professional group you can join that's related to your industry? Sign up and attend meetings to rub elbows with new folks.

Attend Events: Network, network, network! Go to trade shows, open-air markets, speaking events, galas, auctions and more. Find the places the people you want to connect with are likely to be and make an appearance.

Grow Your Network: Introductions are always better when they're made by a friend. Grow your social network online, or better yet, in person, and the introductions will begin pouring in.

YOUR MISSION

This week, your mission is to 'work the room.' Choose an event, meeting, class or other place where you can network with like-minded individuals. Make sure you're presenting yourself well and are in a positive frame of mind. Practice making your entrance and leaving an impression. Join conversations, make connections, get some phone numbers or new followers. This week, put yourself out there and expand your social circle for more effective networking.

6

OVERCOMING CONVERSATION CHALLENGES

"The biggest communication problem is we do not listen to understand. We listen to reply."

— STEPHEN R. COVEY, AUTHOR

Oops. You said the wrong thing. Don't worry, it happens! Every interaction can have its pitfalls, but there's always a way to turn things around. Conversational obstacles can become stepping stones that lead to deeper connections, if you know how to make that happen. Dealing with awkward silences and overcoming barriers takes work, but when you use all of your tools, you can easily turn a negative interaction into a positive one.

DEALING WITH AWKWARD SILENCES

Chirp, chirp, chirp. Are you hearing crickets? One moment the conversation is flowing, and then, for whatever reason, an awkward silence settles in. While each interaction has natural pauses, an awkward silence might occur if that pause goes on too long. It doesn't mean you and your conversational partner are incompatible, only that there might be distraction, shyness, discomfort or embarrassment at play.

Navigating and breaking those awkward silences takes skill and grace, especially if you want to avoid more awkwardness or embarrassment. One of the best ways to move out of this uncomfortable silence is to ask an open-ended question. Unlike closed questions, which will only halt the conversation again, an open-ended question can help you change the subject and restart the rapport you were cultivating.

But what happens if your awkward silence is due to a tense interaction, or a conversation that goes off the rails? In some instances, you might just need to excuse yourself and walk away, but in general, humor can be your best friend for diffusing a bad situation. Even though some people are natural comedians, anyone can be funny by simply employing observational humor. Observe your surroundings and you'll likely find something to joke about. If all else fails, try being self-deprecating, but be sure to know your audience and their limits. Taking jokes too far could turn your awkward silence into a permanent goodbye.

Now that you're mastering some of the skills for learning to talk to anyone, you know that most situations that initially seem like failures are actually opportunities in disguise. Ironically, you can turn an awkward situation into an opportunity for connection, simply by pointing out how awkward you are! One famous awkward silence in film is a scene in *Pulp Fiction*, in which characters Vincent Vega and Mia Wallace are having dinner. It is apparent to the two of them that they are bonding and forming a romantic attraction, but this is strictly taboo. An extended moment of silence passes between them, creating tension, which Mia diffuses simply by pointing out that the awkward silence exists and then quickly changing the subject.

Practice: Have a friend or relative start a mock conversation with you. Ask them to clam up at random and create an awkward silence. Use your skills of observational humor to change the subject and re-start the conversation.

HANDLING DIFFICULT CONVERSATIONS

> *"Sometimes the most important conversations are the most difficult to engage in."*
>
> — JEANNE PHILLIPS, AKA DEAR ABBY, RENOWNED ADVICE COLUMNIST

No one wants to have difficult conversations. It's human nature to want to avoid conflict or disagreements at all cost; after all, these things can be emotionally draining and painful. There can be no resolution, though, without addressing head-on any conflicts you may be experiencing. Here are some tried and true strategies for managing conflict and disagreements that can help you navigate difficult conversations.

Address the Conflict: Problems don't simply disappear. If you previously had a good rapport with someone and now they are giving you the cold shoulder, there may be a reason. Approach them and ask about the problem in a calm tone with a neutral expression, so you keep the situation from escalating further.

Clarify the Issue: Allow plenty of time for the other person to speak their mind. Really listen, and when they've spoken their peace, clarify the issue. Preface your response with, "What I'm hearing from you is…" and then repeat back to them what they said to you so they know you were actively listening.

Identify Solutions: For every problem there is at least one solution. Ask your conversational partner, "What can I do to fix this?" or "Is there a different way?" or "What can I do to help?" Ask questions until you find at least one, if not more, solutions for the problem at hand.

Follow Up: Problem solved, right? Not so fast. Be sure to monitor the situation and follow up to make sure everything is truly settled between the two of you.

It's common for tensions to run high when addressing conflicts. From racing pulses and sweaty palms to adrenaline surges and dry mouth, the physical reactions we feel from conflict are very real. Raising your voice or clamming up will create other negative effects for you and your conversational partner. While it isn't easy to manage conflicts, it's important to stay calm! Use the following techniques to help yourself stay calm and composed when emotions run high.

Anticipate: Knowing to look out for triggers is half the game. If you can see that the conversation is going to a place you aren't quite comfortable with, or if you see that emotions are going to start running high, dial the conversation back.

Take Deep Breaths: Slow down and take a time out with a few deep breaths. Stressful situations make your heart race and cause your breathing to speed up. Forcing yourself to slow down your breathing will tell your body that everything is okay.

Check Your Attitude: Wait… am *I* the drama? Maybe you aren't approaching this conversation the right way. Check your attitude and make sure you aren't adding fuel to the fire with negative facial expressions, closed-off body language or a raised voice. If you're clenching up or find yourself in an intimidating stance, take a time out, relax and try again.

Tensions can often rise during conversation when we discover that the other person has vastly differing opinions from us. This is why staying away from hot button topics like religion and politics is usually advised when meeting someone new. However, some people can't help but bring up sensitive topics that may be offensive to you. Here are some tips for expressing your differing opinion respectfully without having to agree or back down.

Instead of saying, "That's ridiculous," try, "I don't agree, and here's why…"

Instead of saying, "You're wrong," try, "I appreciate your perspective, but I respectfully disagree."

Instead of "That's stupid," say something like, "I see where you're coming from, but I don't agree."

See the pattern here? Top loading your response with a respectful statement helps to create a neutral ground for you to express your disagreement. Depending on the topic, you can simply say "I disagree" and steer the conversation to another topic. If emotions are diffused and you wish to continue hearing each other out, be sure to do so respectfully. Active listening will be essential if you decide to continue with a difficult conversation, especially if you are interested in resolving a conflict or clearing up a misunderstanding.

Difficult conversations are some of the most challenging to have, particularly if you're trying to establish new friendships or expand your network. If you're like me and tend to get a trembling voice or sweaty hands when conflicts arise, practice will be your best bet for overcoming your fears. Slow down, breathe and grab a neutral friend or relative and ask them to do a few dry runs of conversations. Choose topics, like the presidential election, or whether or not aliens are real, that you might discuss with someone who thinks and feels differently than you do. How will you react? What will you say? Remember your reactions to these dry run topics for when a real-life uncomfortable conversation comes your way.

OVERCOMING LANGUAGE BARRIERS

In our global society, we are fortunate to have access to people from all around the world and all walks of life. Whether we are being introduced to a business partner from another country or a new deaf acquaintance, communicating when you don't know each other's language can be difficult. But when people want to get to know each other, language is just another barrier that can be broken down. In the movie *Splash* with Tom Hanks and Daryl Hannah, the two main characters didn't understand each other at first (she spoke mermaid, after all!). However, with perseverance and time (and a lot of lobster), they learned to communicate and understand each other.

Thankfully, there are many non-verbal ways to communicate with people who don't speak the same language as us. Sometimes the barrier is huge, because the person you're speaking with doesn't know any of your language at all. Other times, things like accents or knowing too little of the language can cause confusion. Luckily, with patience and time, you'll almost always be able to figure each other out.

For non-native speakers of your language, be sure to:

Speak slowly and clearly.
Make eye contact.
Use simple language.
Be patient.
Be respectful.
Stay engaged.
Utilize an interpreter if one is available.

Non-verbal communication is the first way to bridge language gaps. Nodding or shaking your head "yes" or "no," respectively, is almost universal, but you can also point or pantomime as needed. Make sure you are being conscious of your facial expression and body language and have an awareness of your own cultural sensitivity.

While it is important to use simple language and to speak slowly, it is also important to ensure that you don't sound patronizing. The other person might not be fluent or may have an invisible disability, so having patience and understanding is crucial. Talking down to someone or mocking their accent will only shut the conversation down. You can help to put non-native speakers of your language at ease or simplify your language without being patronizing by following these steps:

Speak Slowly and Clearly: Take your time and be sure to enunciate your words in a clear, audible voice with an even tone.

Plan Ahead: If you know ahead of time that you are meeting someone from another country, try your hand at learning a few simple greetings or phrases in their language.

Keep It Simple: Don't speak in complex sentences or use uncommon words or slang. For example, instead of asking, "Would you care for a delicious beverage?" simply ask, "Do you want a drink?"

Communicate Visually: Hand gestures, head nods and pantomime can go a long way toward getting your message across. Just make sure that your gestures are appropriate.

Use an App: When all else fails, have a translation app handy on your phone. While the preferred method would be for you not to use your phone and instead remain fully engaged with the person you're speaking with, there are times when spelling it out can be easier.

Language barriers are among the most frustrating obstacles when meeting someone new, but thanks to the modern age, there are many available options to explore that can help you overcome them. Translators and language learning apps can be excellent tools for communicating with people from other countries, especially for complex subjects and ideas. If you know that you will be consistently meeting people who speak a specific language, or if you will be moving to a place where a different language is spoken, learning will be key. Download to your phone one of the many available apps and practice while you're taking a walk, commuting, in the morning while having coffee or at night before turning off the light.

Breaking through language barriers can be tough, but it's always worth it to try. Take the real-life case of author, political activist and disabilities advocate, Helen Keller. Keller was blind and deaf from the time she was 19 months old. Though it was common at the time to institutionalize persons like her, Keller's family was determined to help her and enrolled her in the Perkins School for the Blind. There, she met Anne Sullivan, a visually impaired student who became Keller's instructor. Together, they discovered new ways to communicate, first by tracing letters on the palm of Keller's hand, and eventually, through braille and sign language. With determination and patience, Keller and those who wanted to communicate with her found a way, and Keller went on to be the first deaf and blind person to earn a Bachelor of Arts degree at the age of 24.

NAVIGATING CULTURAL DIFFERENCES

When it comes to navigating cultural differences, our backgrounds and biases can affect how we communicate in many different ways. Culture can affect communication styles, including words, phrases, gestures, tone and of course the language we use. It is important to pay attention to cultural differences, as they can affect how we deliver information, and also how we are perceived by others. Some common cultural barriers in communication include:

- Language barriers
- Ethnocentrism
- Perception and cultural stereotypes
- Lack of cultural knowledge
- Values and beliefs
- Psychological barriers

While it is up to you as the conversational instigator to be as aware as possible of your own prejudices, it's impossible to know everything. You will also be up against others' cultural perceptions of you, and we have very little control over the prejudices of others and the way people perceive us. Even if you make a great entrance, follow all of the etiquette of first impressions and put your best foot forward, there will often be someone who will judge you based on your cultural background.

Here are a few things to remember during cross-cultural meetings:

Be Aware: Being aware of these cultural differences is the first step to overcoming them. If you know you will be meeting someone from a different culture, do your due diligence and research all you can about their customs, especially those that pertain to introductions.

Be Respectful: Doing your research will help you here as well, but just remember that respect goes a long way across all cultures. Learning how to read people, paying attention to body language cues and the setting can help you interpret whether or not your actions or words are insulting anyone.

Ask Questions: If you are confused about something, ask politely for clarification. Be sure that the questions you ask are culturally sensitive and not too intrusive.

Exchange Stories: Humans have been telling each other stories as means of communication since the beginning of time. If they've traveled to where you are, ask how the other person's trip was, and then relay one of your own travel journeys as a way to share common ground.

Think Beyond Race and Ethnicity: A person's culture involves more than their clothing or the color of their skin. Cultivating an interest in other cultures and people will help you better understand where they are coming from.

It isn't always easy to research someone's culture before meeting them. But it is easy to avoid cultural misunderstandings if you follow a few simple, universally appreciated steps.

Keep a Distance: Some cultures appreciate a little space between strangers. Maintain a respectful distance with the person you've just met until you get to know them better. Pay attention to visual cues and body language to see if moving in closer is welcomed.

Address Politely by Name: Use the exact name of the other person that has been given to you. Do not add gendered indicators like "Mr." or "Mrs.," since you will likely not yet know if that is their preferred greeting.

Tone It Down: Keep excited tones, volume and hand gestures to a minimum.

Make Brief Eye Contact: Make eye contact, but only briefly. Some cultures consider too much eye contact to be disrespectful or a threat.

Making friends with someone from another culture can seem intimidating, but it's absolutely possible. There are countless rewards to learning about and forming relationships with people who are different from you. Just take it from Nathan Roberts and

Michael Kimpur. As the two men explained in their TedXRapidCity talk from 2016, forging a successful cross-cultural friendship was powerful and inspiring. Roberts, a suburban man from Minnesota, and Kimpur, a nomadic Kenyan tribal elder, became unlikely best friends who ended up working together! Roberts befriended Kimpur when they were both college students in Minnesota and helped him overcome the culture shock of being in a new country. They quickly established a rapport and shared their lives with each other, as well as their goals for helping others in need. The two men later went on to fund a school together in Kimpur's home country of Kenya.

RECOVERING FROM MISSTEPS

So you've made a misstep… that's okay! There's a reason the miscommunication trope is so popular in books and movies; people have misunderstandings all the time! The good news is that most social missteps can be walked back, as long as you have the tools to do it. Here's how to recover from missteps and gracefully turn around conversational errors:

Decide Whether an Apology Is Necessary: Did you really say the wrong thing? Sometimes pointing out errors can do more harm than good. Take a moment and ask yourself if what you said (or didn't say) really was offensive or detrimental to the conversation. If it seems like someone is waiting for you to add something or explain yourself, then by all means, continue. But if the conversation has moved on from your blunder, then you should do the same.

Acknowledge Your Mistake: Backpedaling is almost always seen as a half-hearted way of saving face. This is why being up front with people and apologizing as soon as possible is your best bet. Taking ownership of your mistakes with a genuine "I'm sorry" is important if you accidentally say something that could be perceived as offensive or rude.

Explain: Explain yourself without making excuses. If the situation calls for it, provide a resolution or a fix for whatever happened. This is your chance to dust yourself off after the apology, and follow up with, "What I meant to say was…"

Carry On: Once you have acknowledged, apologized, and explained yourself, it's time to move on. Bringing the topic up again after making a conversational blunder will only embarrass you and the other person all over again. Change the subject, make a joke or give them a compliment and you may be surprised to find that the whole situation is easily forgotten!

One of the best ways to never make these kinds of mistakes is to learn about them as they happen. Pay attention to social blunders that others make in movies and in real life as well, and note how they are handled. Most importantly, learn to forgive yourself when you make a social blunder. Remember, no one is perfect. Even the most intelligent, sophisticated and self-assured person will make a social blunder now and then. While it's important to not make mistakes from the outset, it's even more important to learn, apologize, and make things right when you do make mistakes. In other words, don't give up after one bad experience. Be resilient and try, try again!

Bonus: Grab a map or globe and randomly select a place in the world. Learn all about their social customs, their language and their culture.

YOUR MISSION

Jump that hurdle! This week, I want you to get out of your comfort zone and try to have those difficult conversations. Is there someone in your personal or professional life with whom you've had a misunderstanding? Have you recently experienced a miscommunication, or do you know someone who doesn't speak the same language as you? Is there a new co-worker in your office who comes from a different background than you? Seek out someone who will challenge your skills as a conversationalist this week and put into action all of the lessons you've just learned.

7

ENCOURAGING OPENNESS IN OTHERS

"Problems can become opportunities when the right people come together."

— ROBERT REDFORD

Getting someone to open up to you is an art form that begins with trust. Fostering openness in a new friend or acquaintance can be instantaneous or can take some time, but either way, the process thrives on empathy. Open conversations flourish in a space of understanding, and this chapter is designed to help you create those settings and set yourself up for success.

CREATING A SAFE SPACE

A room is just a room, right? Think again. In *Ghostbusters 2* is a scene where Dr. Spengler is observing a couple through glass as they wait for their marriage counseling appointment. He explains that he intentionally extends their wait and raises the temperature in the room to see how the couple will react. As you can imagine, more waiting and an uncomfortable environment added friction to an already tense situation, and the waiting couple became even more hostile toward each other.

If your goal is to persuade someone to open up to you, then creating a comfortable environment is crucial. Everything from the color of the walls to the temperature of the room, lighting, noise and seating should all be considered when choosing a location for conversation. While an arcade might be a fun place to hang out, the noise, lights and activity in such a location aren't conducive for meaningful conversation. This is why candlelight, soft music and a private location usually come to mind when we think of a romantic date. Choose a neutral, calm space — like a coffee shop or a quiet park — for an ideal conversational environment.

The way you behave is another thing you can control when it comes to creating a safe space. Showing up with a non-judgmental attitude sets the tone to encourage openness and sharing, especially with someone new. Giving off a vibe of skepticism, judgment or disapproval will only shut down pathways to conversation.

In addition to a calm environment and a good attitude, you'll also need to foster confidentiality and trust in your conversational partners. No one will feel safe with you if you can't keep their secrets! Being able to share sensitive information and know it won't be shared with others is an essential way to cultivate deeper connections and help someone truly open up to you.

Responding appropriately during the conversation will also help your new friend or acquaintance feel safe around you. Being able to respond genuinely and with empathy is key to encouraging further sharing. Once again, here are a few phrases you can use to respond empathetically during conversations.

"What can I do to help?"
"I'm sorry you're dealing with this."
"I can see how that would be uncomfortable/hard/difficult."
"I'm here if you need me."
"I'm happy to listen whenever you need me."
"That sounds upsetting/awful/challenging."

Using correct body language is another way to signal openness and willingness to listen. If your face and words say one thing, but your body language says another, the person you are speaking with may not give you their full trust. Remember to keep your shoulders relaxed, practice mirroring their body language, and avoid using overly exaggerated motions. Making someone feel "at home" in your presence isn't difficult if you look at the big picture and are careful to create an environment that feels safe and welcoming.

THE ART OF SUBTLE INQUIRY

There's a fine line between wanting to learn more about someone and seeming downright nosy. When it comes to meeting someone new and learning about them, subtlety is key. Whether you're trying to get to know someone on a first date or for business purposes, diving into too-personal topics too soon can be off-putting. Below are some ways to get someone to open up to you on their comfort level and in their own time without seeming overbearing.

Ask Open-Ended Questions: Practice asking questions that invite your new acquaintance or friend to elaborate rather than give yes or no answers. This allows the person to drive how much information they want to share, while still keeping the conversation flowing. Here are a few examples of how to turn a closed question into an open-ended question.

Closed: "Do you like to travel?"
Open: "What has been your favorite place to travel to?"

Closed: "Do you like animals?"
Open: "What is your favorite animal and why?"

Closed: "Do you like music?"
Open: "What bands/performers/kinds of music do you like?"

Closed: "Isn't real life funny sometimes?"
Open: "Do you have a funny real life story?"

Closed: "Do you have any hobbies?"
Open: "What are your hobbies?"

The point of asking open-ended questions is to help guide the person you're speaking with to open up about themselves. This also helps to build stronger connections and makes for a more memorable encounter because they will feel as though you are truly interested in them.

Display Active Listening Cues: As you continue to ask open-ended questions and keep your conversation flowing, be sure to practice your active listening cues. Use non-verbal and verbal affirmation, like eye contact, nodding and responding with words of agreement to show you are engaged. Be sure to keep the following points in mind:

- Stay focused; don't become distracted.
- Face the speaker; retain eye contact.
- Don't offer your solutions or opinions.
- Don't interrupt; allow them to finish.
- Listen without passing judgment.
- Don't be thinking about what you'll say when they stop talking.

- Ask follow-up questions to stay engaged.

Balance Sharing and Inquiry: As mentioned earlier in our discussion of rapport, conversations are like a game of table tennis. While there needs to be some back and forth movement to keep the conversation flowing, there's still a delicate balance between asking questions and sharing personal stories. Mutual exchange works best when everyone has a seat at the table and enough equal time to say what they have to say and be heard. Consider whether you're doing too much talking, or not enough. Memorable conversations happen when the person you're speaking with feels valued and heard, so if you are only talking about yourself, then you'll be remembered in an unfavorable way.

Read Their Cues: Sometimes a person just isn't in the mood to chat, and that's okay! Remember that you want your exchanges to be memorable in a positive way; you never want to intentionally make someone feel uncomfortable. Reading people's verbal and non-verbal cues becomes easier with practice, but here are a few clues to help you decide whether someone is open to talking or whether they're ready to exit the conversation.

Open to Talk:

- Smiling
- Calm facial expression
- Maintaining eye contact
- Focused
- Calm body language
- Faced toward you
- Nodding
- Using engaging language (open-ended answers)

Needs Space:

- Frowning
- Tense, furrowed facial expression
- Tense body language; arms crossed, shoulders rigid
- Face away from you or toward the door
- Not maintaining eye contact
- Distracted
- Using clipped, closed language (yes/no answers)

Timing and Pace: Now that you know how to read someone's vibe, it's important to pay attention to the timing of your questions. The longer your conversation, the more rapport you build, and the more in-depth questions you can ask. Deep conversation comes from asking tough questions, but you can't ask them right away. Once you are certain that the person you are speaking with is at ease and once you have shared some sensitive information about yourself, you can begin to dip your toes into deeper conversational waters. Remember to ask open-ended questions and listen without passing judgment. Pause and allow time for reflection in between these tough questions, but most importantly, allow them to respond in their own way and in their own time.

EMPATHETIC LISTENING

"People don't really listen, they just wait for their turn to talk."

— CHUCK PALAHNIUK, AMERICAN NOVELIST

One thing that will truly make your conversational skills stand out is learning to be an empathetic listener. I think that most people have felt, at one time or another, that they just want to be heard. When I think about my own conversations with friends and family, I often leave feeling relieved that someone just listened without offering judgment, opinions or solutions. Many people don't understand what it means to be an empathetic listener, and think they need to "fix" whatever problem or situation is presented to them in order to be helpful. In reality, many of us simply need to vent and feel as though we are being heard.

Understanding vs. Solving: You can be an empathetic person, but forget how to be an empathetic listener. When someone presents a hardship or problem to us, often our knee-jerk reaction is to offer a solution. In reality, this method is usually off-putting and doesn't really help. Unless someone has explicitly asked you for your opinion or you have a viable solution, it's best to keep those thoughts to yourself. You can still help guide them through their problem or situation by showing understanding instead of attempting to solve it. Here's how to tell the difference:

Mary wants to move in with her boyfriend, but she can't bring her dog with because he is allergic. This situation leaves her feeling sad and torn about what to do.

Solving: "Why don't you ask your boyfriend to take allergy medicine? Or maybe give the dog to a friend?"
Understanding: "That's a really tough decision to make. I'm sure you love your dog and your boyfriend and don't want to choose between them."

Paraphrasing and Reflecting: Another way you can practice empathetic listening is through paraphrasing and reflecting. In paraphrasing, you repeat back the sentiments that were expressed to you in a different way to show that you were listening. In reflecting, you go beyond repetition and help identify some of the emotions or feelings that the person might have been experiencing. For example, take this situation:

Sam tells you he was in a car accident last month and his car was totaled.

Paraphrasing Response: "A car accident! I'm so sorry, it's awful that your car was totaled."
Reflecting: "I'm so sorry to hear you were in an accident! You must have been so scared and upset."

Paraphrasing is a perfectly fine response in a conversation. However, if you wish to show greater empathy, choose reflective statements. Consider how the situation would make you or someone else feel? What would you want someone to say to you? Mirror those sentiments back to the other person to show that you understand. This brings us to our next point.

Recognizing Emotions: Sometimes, it's not what someone says but how they say it. Sometimes the people we speak to can be hard to read; perhaps they are stoic by nature or have lived a life that causes them to mask their emotions. Have you ever spoken to someone and been unable to tell if what they were saying was good or bad, simply because of their delivery? You can still recognize and respond to the way people speak about certain things based on body language, facial expressions, and tone of voice. Consider the following:

You are meeting your friend Sandra for coffee. She flops down in her seat, sighs, and offers you a tight-lipped smile. "I just found out I'm getting a promotion."

Do you think Sandra is happy about getting a promotion? I would guess not, or if she is, she's feeling conflicted. In such a case, you have the opportunity to ask questions and prod her to open up. Possible follow-up questions might be:

"How do you feel about that?"
"Tell me more."
"Is that something you wanted?"

Evaluate the other person's response and let them lead the conversation. If they appear to be too stressed, you can always ask if they want to change the subject to something more pleasant. Avoid interrupting them to ensure they are able to fully express themselves before moving on from the topic at hand.

Validate Feelings: One of the best ways to come across as an empathetic listener is to leave your conversational partner feeling validated. You don't necessarily have to agree with the other person, but let them know they've been heard. Refer back to Chapter Four: Rapid Rapport-Building Techniques to brush up on your validation skills, if needed!

BUILDING TRUST

Building and maintaining trust is the #1 factor in all successful relationships. Whether it's a platonic, romantic, or business relationship, being trustworthy is essential in fostering meaningful connections. Consistency, reciprocity, reliability, confidentiality and respecting boundaries goes a long way toward ensuring you're the kind of person someone wants to put their faith in.

Be Consistent: Do what you say, when you say it. If you promise to walk the dog at a certain time every day, or drop off the mail at a certain time every day, be sure to do it. Following through shows you are a trustworthy person and helps to put the person you're building a relationship with at ease.

Share Experiences: Sharing is caring. When you entrust someone with sensitive information about yourself, you encourage others to open up about themselves. When information is only passed one way, it can leave the other person feeling vulnerable and untrusting of you.

Respect Boundaries: Does the person you're speaking with prefer to use a certain pronoun? Do they seem reserved and not interested in sharing more with you? Always take their boundaries into consideration, change your approach or take a step back, if needed.

Show Interest: Distracted people tend not to be trustworthy. When you show genuine interest, your conversational partners will believe that you are truly invested in what they have to say. Why would someone share information with you if you don't seem to care? Be genuine and stay engaged.

Be Reliable: Confidentiality is vital. Treat all of your conversations with confidentiality. As we discussed earlier, you might be tempted to share juicy conversational tidbits with a friend or spouse, but fight the urge! You never know who is talking to whom, or who knows whom. Zipped lips are trustworthy lips!

RESPECTING BOUNDARIES

Personal boundaries vary from one person to another, but they are crucial to recognize when fostering relationships. Some folks are better at speaking up for themselves regarding their boundaries and limits, but others don't know how and end up suffering in silence. Empathetic individuals are very good at reading people and are cognizant of respecting boundaries. Read on to see how you can improve your skills at reading people and discover if you understand what it means to recognize the limitations of others.

Recognizing Personal Limits: Our world is full of different individuals with different abilities, needs, loves, fears and… well, differences. What may seem normal to you, like running errands, could trigger a full-blown panic attack in another person. This is where reading people's emotions, expressions and body language can be your superpower. If you are in conversation with someone and the topic has shifted, be mindful of the expressions, body language and responses of the other person. If they were previously open and chatty, but seem to have suddenly clammed up, this is a sign that they are uncomfortable with the new topic.

Graceful Topic Changes: So you've noticed that your conversational partner has become uncomfortable. How do you change the topic without embarrassing them or making them even more uncomfortable? In Chapter 6: Overcoming Conversation Challenges, we discussed how to break away from awkward silences. The same rules apply here, except you need to make note of the conversation topic and take care not to bring it up again. Consider making a joke to lighten the mood and relax your conversational partner again before diving into another topic.

Responding to Discomfort: Whether or not someone is expressing through verbal or non-verbal responses that they are uncomfortable and their boundaries have been crossed, it is your job to address their concerns. The worst thing you can do is dismiss them and continue speaking, especially if you know they aren't at ease. As with most things, apologies go a long way! Even if you aren't uncomfortable, or if you don't agree with the person, apologizing will help display your respect and can serve as a jumping-off point for moving on.

Ask Permission: We know the personal topics to avoid in conversations, especially with people we don't know well — religion, politics, etc. If you are itching to have a deep conversation about a controversial topic, or if you feel as though the conversation is heading in that direction, then it is always polite to ask. It's not easy to know what might offend someone, especially if you don't know them well, but most people have a good idea of what's taboo and what isn't.

Cultural Sensitivity: Remember that some cultures prefer personal physical distance during conversations. Standing too close, touching, or maintaining intense eye contact could be crossing their boundaries. In some cultures, speaking about certain deities or mythological creatures might be out of bounds. Furthermore, calling someone by the wrong name or the incorrect gender marker can create a wall that is hard to break down. Remember that cultural gaffes happen and apologies can be made, but educating yourself beforehand is always best. When in doubt, ask permission, and if needed, adjust your behavior accordingly.

YOUR MISSION

This week, I want you to get someone out of their shell. Pinpoint someone you would like to know better and try developing a deeper connection with them. Use empathetic listening, ask questions with subtlety, and make an effort to create a safe space for them. Make notes about how your interactions played out. What could you do better in the future? What worked best? In the coming weeks, continue to show that you are trustworthy by following through and sharing more personal information about yourself while taking care to respect their boundaries.

8

BECOMING A CONVERSATION MAGNET

"Good conversation is as stimulating as black coffee, and just as hard to sleep after."

— ANNE MORROW LINDBERGH, AMERICAN WRITER, AVIATOR, AND WIFE OF CHARLES LINDBERGH

Being charismatic in conversation is like creating a spark in the dark – learn to ignite it, and you'll light up every interaction with warmth and interest. Some people just seem to be born oozing charisma; they have the ability to make you feel as though they are speaking directly to you, as if you're the only person in the room. Charisma can be a learned skill, as long as you have confidence and are willing to put yourself out there.

CHARISMATIC COMMUNICATION

There are people who are outgoing and there are people who are magnetic, but how can you tell if someone is charismatic? These are people who can grab and hold the attention of a single person or an entire crowd. Charismatic people can be persuasive and influential, sometimes to the detriment of others. Being charismatic doesn't mean you are necessarily a good person, because in the hands of criminals, corrupt politicians, and cult leaders, charisma is the tool they use to gain followers. However, when in the hands of an honest person with good intentions, charisma can help you widen your reach and expand your circle of business partners and friends.

Charismatic individuals are:

- Empathetic
- Humble
- Present
- Generous
- Vulnerable
- Altruistic
- Interested in everyone
- Non-narcissistic
- Humorous
- Kind

One way charismatic individuals captivate and get people to pay attention to them is through voice modulation. By varying their pitch, tone and volume, these people can make their voice more engaging. Anyone who has sat through a speech given by someone with a monotonous tone can tell you how disinteresting their experience was. Check out these tips for making your speaking voice more engaging and… well, charismatic!

Speak Loud and Clear: Somewhere between your normal speaking voice and shouting is the perfect pitch. Good posture, with shoulders back, chin up and even breathing will help you enunciate and be heard in a crowd.

Emphasize Powerful Words: Take effective pauses in your speech after specific words to help drive home your point. This will help your speech sound more interactive and create intrigue to keep your audience listening.

Press Pause: Take effective pauses after emphasizing certain words or ideas. Use this time to make eye contact, adjust your posture or ensure your facial expressions match your tone.

Pauses give your listeners time to digest what you're saying before you move on to the next idea.

Be Enthusiastic: Confidence and enthusiasm are often contagious when speaking to others. When listeners see how enthusiastic you are about your topic, it encourages them to become equally enthusiastic.

HUMOR AND WIT

When all else fails, having a good sense of humor can have a big impact. Consider your favorite stand-up comedians; being on stage and telling jokes requires plenty of confidence and charm! While a sense of humor is a skill all its own, below are a few tips you might follow to begin developing a witty personality.

Understanding Your Audience: As always, keep your audience in mind when cracking jokes. If you are in a professional setting, keep your humor clean and try to tailor it to your audience. Knowing the types of people in the crowd will help your jokes land and also save you from embarrassment.

Timing and Delivery: Much like with voice modulation, it's not always about what you say, but how you say it that makes something funny.

TYPES OF HUMOR

Deadpan: Dry, deadpan humor is ideal for almost any situation because of its casual tone. With this type of humor, it's important to tell a funny story with a straight face and monotone to ensure it lands effectively. Next time you tell a story that you know is funny, try to deliver it with a straight face and see what kind of reaction you get!

Self-Deprecating: Taking shots at yourself instead of others helps you appear witty and self-aware. No one likes to be made fun of, but when we make fun of ourselves, we tend to seem more relatable and our listeners are more likely to pay attention.

Self-Enhancing Humor: Just like self-deprecating humor, this type of humor shows you're self-aware. For example, actress Sofia Vergara was teased by an interviewer about her accent. Instead of striking back negatively, she instead pretended she had received a compliment, and suggested the interviewer was "jealous" of her accent. Vergara used self-enhancing humor to positively turn around negative comments about her accent.

One-Liners: Short and sweet. One-liners are a great way to break the ice and start out your conversation with everyone laughing. Consider keeping a running log on your phone or in a notepad of one-liners you can use in any situation. Make sure they're clean, universal and a little silly, like these examples:

"I was going to wear my camo print pants, but I couldn't find them."
"Never trust atoms, they make up everything."
"I didn't expect orthopedic shoes would help, but I stand corrected."

Anecdotal Humor: Sharing anecdotes is a great way to be humorous without telling jokes or poking fun at yourself or anyone else. Think of situations that are relatable, like buying a $7 coffee and immediately spilling it on your white shirt. Injecting your conversation with a little bit of levity can help others view you as open, funny and easy to relate to.

Slapstick Humor: Jim Carey, a king of slapstick humor, uses exaggerated facial expressions and body movements to get his laughs. While this type of humor is inventive and works for those who know how to master it, slapstick doesn't work well in all environments.

Dark Humor: Just remember, this type of humor can be disturbing and full of taboos. Know your audience well before diving into dark humor, as some people don't appreciate or "get" it. Dark humor doesn't have to include aggression or shock, but should be used with great care.

Satirical Humor: It's funny because it's true! Much like self-deprecating humor, satirical humor pokes fun at humanity's flaws. This type of humor works best when you know your audience and can master timing, simply by stating what everyone else is thinking.

LEAVING A LASTING IMPRESSION

When was the last time you met someone memorable? Were they wearing something unique? Did they tell a joke that was really funny? Did they make you feel special in a certain way?

In the film *Citizen Kane*, the character Bernstein recalls seeing a girl in a white dress with a parasol on a ferry many years earlier. He said that he only saw her for a second, but that not a month had gone by his entire life when he didn't think about that girl. While this sentiment deals in themes of memory, loss and idealism, at the core Bernstein was left with a lasting impression. At that moment in his life, the girl in white with the parasol embodied all of his dreams and desires, and imprinted on him in a very powerful way.

The words we say and the things we do affect not only the way people perceive us, but whether or not they remember us. When we meet new people, it is up to us to ensure that we leave a lasting impression. When you say goodbye, it is your goal to leave the other person hungry for more and wanting to meet up with you again. Crafting a memorable conversation is an art form that can be learned and honed with time and practice. All of the things we have discussed up to this point, from making an impression to being charismatic and funny, will help you become an impressive conversationalist. While appearing nice and being personable will certainly help, in the end, leaving a lasting impression comes from taking a few small steps.

Start with Small Talk: Some may dismiss small talk, but initial exchanges and conversations that may seem meaningless help to build rapport. You can't just barge into a conversation or chat up someone new with the big, deep stuff first. Take your time and start small. Think about it as a warm-up for bigger things to come!

Talk about Unique Topics: I enjoy collecting weird and interesting facts and sharing them with others. (Hey, did you know that sloths can hold their breath longer than dolphins? It's true!) Interjecting unique facts and topics into conversation will not only make people smile, but it will help you to seem more interesting and memorable. Keep a running mental list of some interesting and funny facts to share the next time you encounter an awkward pause or need an icebreaker.

Personal Branding: What is it about you that makes you... well, *you?* Some of the most memorable celebrities have their own personal branding, whether it's the way they speak, the way they dress or the things they do. Celebrities like Dolly Parton stand out with lavish costumes and their sparkly style, while other celebs like Fran Drescher are known for their distinctive voice. You don't have to put on a show at every interaction, but consider how you can incorporate your own personal branding into conversations.

Utilize Storytelling: Are you the shark expert guy? Or do you really, really like 80s techno music? Make yourself stand out by having your own memorable brand of expertise woven into your storytelling. As we've discussed before, great storytelling can help to carry a conversation and keep things flowing. But if the story you're telling is boring (like how your car insurance rates just went up) you'll elicit the opposite effect of the one you're going for. Consider marrying your personal branding techniques with storytelling and humor to really give your new acquaintances or friends a taste of your true personality.

Follow-Up and Continuity: Now that you've got their attention, how do you hold it? Following up after memorable conversations is the best way to keep your new friend or acquaintance in the loop. If you exchanged phone numbers or business cards, shoot them a text or an email after a few days have passed. If you follow each other on social media, continue to use your "brand" to display your personality in your posts and when you comment on their posts. If things are going well, arrange another in-person meet up in the future!

CULTIVATING CURIOSITY

One complaint that people tend to have when they're learning to talk to anyone is that they perceive themselves as boring. "I don't have anything good to talk about!" or "No one will think I'm interesting!" Sound familiar? As the old saying goes, 'if you're bored, then you're boring,' and no one wants to be a big snooze. Humans are curious by nature, but if you feel like you don't have anything to talk about, then perhaps the solution is for you to cultivate your curiosity. I get it; work, home life and the world in general can leave us feeling flat and worn down. But there's a great big world out there to get lost in with new things to discover every day. Follow along and I'll show you how to recapture your enthusiasm for learning and discovering new things!

Stay Informed: It's hard to keep up with conversations about the latest trends and world news if you have your head stuck in the sand. You don't have to spend hours pouring over every media outlet and you can't be expected to know everything, of course. Choose a reliable news source, either an online newspaper or morning show, and make a habit of reading or watching in the morning with coffee (or your favorite beverage). With video streaming, more information than ever is widely available for free with the touch of a button, so seek out documentaries on topics you are interested in. Make TV time learning time and dive into an educational program now and then.

Ask Questions: No one knows everything. One of the best ways for us to learn is by asking questions. During conversation, asking questions is a great way to get people to open up, so long as the questions are appropriate and don't cross any boundaries. You'll learn something new, and your conversational partner will feel like you're engaged because you've asked about their life and interests.

Practice Active Listening: Are you paying attention? By now I hope that all your conversations involve active listening and that you're giving your conversational partners your full attention. Active listening is also essential for helping you to gain knowledge and expand your own horizons. Consider learning about someone new in the same way you would in school studying for a test. The more laser-focused you are, the more information you'll retain.

Encourage Others to Share: Much like asking questions, nudging your conversational partners to share can be a learning experience that helps to strengthen bonds. If you're naturally reserved like me, try the following:

Expand Your Interests: Got some free time? Join new clubs, whether that means taking up martial arts or learning Cajun cooking. It is never too late to join an adult tap dancing class, to learn conversational French or join a kite sailing club. Book clubs, pickleball, yoga, or art classes are all easy ways to expand your horizons, learn new skills or simply get out there and have some enjoyable experiences. Having new experiences is the best way to meet new people and accumulate interesting things to talk about!

VERSATILITY IN TOPICS

So you've started to expand your horizons, look into new hobbies or interests, and pay more attention to what's going on in the world. Wonderful! While it might be tempting to laser focus your efforts on only one or two specific interests, the best way to talk to a variety of different people is to diversify your subject areas. You might be interested in talking about European post-war art for hours on end, but the person you're conversing with might not be interested at all. It's up to you to figure out which topics work with your new acquaintances if your goal is to keep the conversation flowing.

Identifying Common Interests: When you've caught someone's attention, it's important to keep it. Ideally, you'll be able to quickly identify common interests you have with your conversational partner so they will remain engaged. Scan their wardrobe and outward appearance for clues (without being creepy!) and see if you can guess what they're interested in. Ask open-ended questions and let them give you even more clues about their families, hobbies and interests.

Adapting to Different Audiences: So you're at a pharmaceutical convention, but you don't know the first thing about medicine or prescriptions. How do you adapt? Chances are, even if the audience you're in is one you're not familiar with, many of the people there will still have similar interests as you. Asking open-ended questions with a touch of humor can help you weed out some and find the people who will want to engage in conversation with you. A question like "What do you like to do on your days off?" should encourage anyone to open up, regardless of who they are.

Diving Deep: Forging deeper connections happens when we are able to find that common ground. Once you've flitted from light topics such as what kind of food and music you both like and what kind of sports you play, how do you segue into topics that go beneath the surface? You can transition smoothly from talking about cat toys to long-term career goals by simply asking questions. Once you've used your skills of deduction, read their body language, and gotten to know them a bit, feel free to ask those open-ended questions that can lead to deeper conversation about career, family, beliefs, values and more.

Handling Challenging Topics: What happens when your topics become too versatile? Often when we are speaking with someone new, we can find ourselves caught off guard and before we know it, controversial topics come up. Don't shy away from them! While this is tricky, if done well, discussing deep, life-altering subjects can help you forge a bond that can turn someone into a life-long friend. Even if you don't fully agree, be sure that the other person is heard with verbal affirmations like "I understand." Also ask your new acquaintance or friend if they feel comfortable continuing to talk about potentially sensitive topics. They'll appreciate being able to give their consent and will respect you for asking.

Encourage Curiosity in Others: Don't keep your newfound passion for learning to yourself. Share your interests openly and encourage your new friends to look into your hobbies or pastimes for themselves. Use your new experiences as a segue for asking questions like, "Have you ever been hang-gliding?" or "Did you know that you need a dozen eggs to bake a pound cake?" Share your passions and the things you've learned with others and you'll be surprised at how easily the conversation will flow.

YOUR MISSION

Study time! Develop a daily habit of reading the news, researching new topics and finding interesting things to talk about. Investigate your local rec center for low-cost classes you can take. Visit the library and pick up books on topics you've never studied before, or check out places in your city you've never been to before. Getting out, having experiences and exposing yourself to new things will almost certainly help you become a more interesting, well-rounded conversationalist!

9

MASTERING DIGITAL COMMUNICATION

"I'm a great believer that any tool that enhances communication has profound effects in terms of how people can learn from each other, and how they can achieve the kind of freedoms that they're interested in."

— BILL GATES

Some of you reading this guide will be old enough to remember a time before emails, text messages and social media. Like so many other areas of progress, digital conversations change faster than we ever could have expected, and continue to evolve today. Our online world allows us to make friends and do business with folks all over the world, but as a result, our digital conversations often outnumber face-to-face interactions. While getting to know someone in person is preferred, sometimes time and location constraints make that impossible. Mastering the art of online communication isn't just useful, it's essential. Think you've got the bases of digital communication covered? Read on to learn all you need to consider to effectively connect with new friends around the world.

THE ETIQUETTE OF TEXT MESSAGING

Text messages are quick, convenient, and often confusing. While texting someone with whom you are intimate and familiar, like a partner, parent, or child can be casual and full of inside jokes, emojis and memes, this approach doesn't work with everyone. Review these essential messaging etiquette points to see if your text communication is as effective as when you're speaking IRL.

Keep It Short and Sweet: Make your communications clear and succinct. Text format is limited, and you don't want to bombard someone with an entire page and multiple paragraphs of words. Brevity and clarity are key.

Watch Your Tone: I'm so excited! Whoa, easy there, new text message friend. If you're using exclamation points after every texted sentence, you may need to take it down a notch. Just as when you're speaking to someone, the tone of your text messages is also important. Keep exclamation points to a minimum, and reserve them for true exclamations, such as "Congratulations!" or "Happy Birthday!"

Emoji Use: Emojis; to use them or not to use them, that is the question. Much like slang words and acronyms, emojis should be used with extreme care and kept to a minimum. It is important to note that even something as innocent as a friendly smile emoji or a heart emoji may be misconstrued, so know your audience. The meaning of emojis' changes from person to person and some that may seem innocent (like a certain vegetable) might have *Not Safe for Work* undertones. Emojis are fun to use, but it isn't worth it to send a stream of them to confuse or potentially turn off someone new. Don't worry, when you get to know your friend or acquaintance better, you'll be able to fire off all the emojis you like!

Timing and Response: There's something off-putting about receiving a text from someone you hardly know at an awkward time, like in the middle of the night. Keep your texts to new friends or acquaintances to daylight hours. Response time is also essential to keep in mind; if someone is waiting for an answer from you, try to respond as soon as you can. On the other hand, you shouldn't feel obligated to respond immediately if it's not something you're prepared to answer. Finally, consider waiting a while after meeting someone before texting them, but not too long or they may forget who is texting them unless you identify yourself!

Group Text Dynamics: Wandering through the bog of group texts can be a nightmare. When the group text is chatty, it can be hard to get a word in edgewise. If there is something you specifically want to address, make sure to "reply" just to that text and not to the entire random chain. If things become too intense in a group text, you can always opt out and invite the person you want to speak to into a text chat on the side.

Privacy and Discretion: Sharing sensitive or private information can leave someone feeling very vulnerable. It's important to keep what's said between you and your conversational partner confidential if you ever hope for them to open up to you again. It may be tempting to share salacious information with your partner, best friend or parents, but to ensure true discretion, always keep your word and keep your lips zipped!

MASTERING EMAIL COMMUNICATION

Remember writing letters by hand, folding them and placing them in an envelope, affixing a postage stamp and sending it in the mail? What once was a commonplace way of sending communication to our friends, relatives and potential business partners is now a novelty for most. While emails are more convenient, faster and more accessible in many ways, writing them is a skill all its own. While most of us know our way around an email inbox these days, the etiquette for writing an email is still lost on some. Follow along and learn the essentials of mastering email communication.

Effective Subject Lines: The first step to getting someone to read your email is to ensure they open it! Much like junk mail, some emails end up going directly into the trash folder. Don't let yours suffer this fate. When coming up with an effective subject line, keep the following guidelines in mind:

Personalize It: Use the recipient's name, and add something you know about them to attract their attention.

Keep It Short: With subject lines, less is better. Don't let your message be cut off!

Be Specific: What is this email about? Don't beat around the bush.

Ask Questions: Consider asking a question that will intrigue the reader, spurring them to open the email.

The rules of letter writing and email writing are very similar at their core when it comes to structure and clarity. Unlike the olden days, we no longer have to add the date at the top right hand corner, as emails already log that information for you. Some people choose to have informational footers and sign-off signatures automated into their emails for a uniform, professional look every time. Whatever you choose, be sure to format your emails for structure and clarity, above all else. Keep your paragraphs short and to the point (no more than five sentences each) and use a standard font, such as Ariel or Times New Roman, and font size 10 or 12 point, and avoid using fancy script or colored text, as these can be difficult to read on a computer screen.

As with texting, keeping your tone professional is imperative when sending emails. Once you've gotten to know someone, a casual tone is more acceptable, but until then, keep etiquette in mind. Unless you are certain of someone's pronoun or preferred salutations, avoid using gendered prefixes like Mr./Mrs./Miss. Depending on your preference, you can start your email with "Dear" or simply the person's name. Sign off with something simple, like "Sincerely" or "Thank You" and your full name. Overall, stay away from slang, emojis, over-use of punctuation, jokes and rambling thoughts so your emails look polished and professional. Also, don't forget to consider the email address that you use when corresponding with others. Your college email TwilightFan2009@website.net won't seem professional to prospective employers, for example. In the business world, it's best to use your full name for your email address, without extra numbers or flourishes, so it's easy to remember.

So now you've sent your email to a new friend, acquaintance or business connection… how long do you wait to follow up? The general rule is to wait 3-5 business days until you hear back from someone before giving them a little nudge. If you sent an email on Monday, for example, then it's perfectly acceptable to follow up on Friday, if you haven't yet received a response. Keep your follow-up message short, sweet and to the point, and then wait again. After a second 3-5 day cycle, feel free to follow up one last time (politely, of course) and if you don't hear back after that, let it go. No response is a response in itself, and someone who isn't responsive isn't worth your time.

Another obstacle when it comes to composing and answering emails is inbox overload. There are two types of people: those who have empty email inboxes, and those who have hundreds of emails. Guess which people have the most organized, effective communication? If you find it difficult to keep your emails from getting lost, you can prioritize them in the following ways:

Set up a new email account. This is especially important if you have a business or some other professional outlet. Create a new email that's only for business purposes or corresponding with friends, to cut down on the clutter. If your current email is the one you prefer to keep, be sure to unsubscribe to emails and newsletters that no longer serve you. Depending on which email provider you use, you can also organize emails into folders, set up notifications and filters and flag certain emails.

IMPACTFUL SOCIAL MEDIA INTERACTIONS

Social media; love it or hate it, it's here to stay. While the various social media platforms available online can be a minefield for some, for others, they're an essential tool to engage with like-minded people. Whether you want to keep up with family and friends, meet new people with similar interests, or discover something new, social media has a little something for everyone. At its core, social media is… well, social, and implies conversation. To make those conversations impactful on your social media platforms, keep these tips in mind:

Personal Branding: Who are you as a person? The way you portray yourself online should tell your followers and friends almost everything they need to know. From the colors you use, the images and memes you display and the content you post, your followers should be able to understand your personality. Post articles, books, songs, movies and more to share your interests with others and find like-minded people. Tell jokes. Tell stories. Be you!

Create Engaging Posts: Everyone loves a picture of a cute dog or cat, right? While those kinds of posts definitely get clicks and likes, cute pet pics won't always work. To engage like-minded persons with your social posts, you need to know your audience. Be authentic and tell a story, much like you would in person when you're working the room. Pay attention to current social media trends and plan your content around them. Visuals and hashtags will also help to drive interest to your posts and set your words apart. Try using polls or calls to action, like asking a question to keep your followers engaged.

Comment and Reply: The algorithm on social media works best when you engage with others. You can do this by commenting and replying to other people online. Just like with text messaging and emails, approach these interactions in a straightforward, professional and concise way. Be positive and constructive, and don't offer advice unless someone has asked for it. Avoid slang and emojis until you find yourself regularly engaging with that person and have a better feel for how they connect best online with others.

Build Relationships: Can you really build a relationship with someone you only know online? Yes! On a personal note, I've met some of my favorite people and best friends through online interactions. Forging these relationships organically was important to me, and came about through a combination of time, attention and intention. I made sure to interact with the posts of people I liked, boosted their content, and offered positive comments. After some time, I was able to comfortably send my online friends direct messages, in which we would open up and share with one another. If this is your goal, be sure to take things slow, and avoid "love bombing" someone from the get-go. Don't jump into their direct messages right away and begin asking overly personal questions. Stay positive, consistent, and most of all, genuine to who you really are and the online friendships will follow!

Handle Negative Interactions: Yikes. Whether you're dealing with negative feedback, criticism or trolls, the dark side of social media will eventually rear its ugly head. It's up to you to handle those situations with grace. Here's how:

Filter and Block: If someone is consistently trolling you or sending bad energy, feel free to block them. It's your online world and you get to control who has access to it. Also, if certain topics upset you or don't bring you joy, you can filter keywords out of your social media feed. You might even want to set your account to private, if needed.

Don't Feed the Trolls: Simply don't engage with social media accounts that are only there to breed negativity and division. The more you interact with them, the more your blood pressure will rise, and you'll only help raise their algorithm in return.

Document and Report: If someone is continually harassing you, screen shot those interactions. Report those accounts to social media admins to make sure no one else is targeted.

Monitor Your Accounts: Don't let your page run rampant with bots, trolls or fake accounts. Be diligent about who you follow, who you allow to follow you, and who you let have access to your space.

EFFECTIVE VIDEO CALL COMMUNICATION

With telecommuting the norm now for many, video calls have become more common than ever. We use video calls to conduct interviews, team meetings and so much more. However, ensuring effective video call communication is vital if you want to maintain a professional appearance and clearly impart your message.

Technical problems are often at the heart of video call miscommunication. Make sure your audio and video gear is working and up-to-date well ahead of any meeting, and ensure your internet connection is working well, too. Try to conduct your call in a quiet room free from ambient noise like talking, television, or barking dogs. Use good lighting, natural or a ring light, if possible, and consider the background of your video call. There are programs that create a "green screen" effect if the room you are using isn't presentable or if you don't want people to see the interior of your home.

As with all in-person interactions, our appearance is important on video calls. Dress and present yourself just as you would if you were communicating face-to-face (pants optional, but encouraged!). It's also important to be mindful of your body language and expressions while on camera. While maintaining eye contact isn't possible, you can still show that you are engaged, with squared shoulders, a neutral or smiling expression, and nods.

Things can become chaotic on group calls. If you are facilitating a group call, it's important to make sure that all points are covered in a timely manner and that all involved feel heard. Utilize "raised hands" or another method to tag folks into the conversation. Also be mindful of those who may not be chiming in and ask if they have anything to contribute. Above all, be mindful not to veer off the subject, be considerate of everyone's time and don't go over the prescribed time.

Etiquette during video calls is a little different than it is in real life. When you're not speaking, be sure to mute your audio so everyone on the call doesn't have to hear the traffic outside your window, the dog barking in the other room or other ambient noise. Ensure that your camera is positioned in a way that is both flattering to you and ensures that you can properly show your engaged body language and facial expressions. Also be sure to pay attention to the call and unless you are taking notes, don't become distracted with your phone or fidget with something off camera. Video calls can be uncomfortable or more awkward than in-person meetings, but they still provide a useful way to engage with others.

BALANCING DIGITAL AND FACE-TO-FACE INTERACTION

Sometimes we have the option of speaking with our acquaintances or friends either online or in person. Each mode of communication has value, but it isn't always easy to know when a digital meeting or a face-to-face meeting is appropriate. Often in business meetings, it's best to meet in person at first if time, money and location permit. Of course it's possible to get to know someone through digital means, but meeting in person makes things feel more... personal.

If you're meeting someone in person for the first time after knowing them online, transitioning between modes may feel awkward at first. It might feel like meeting them for the first time, or like you're finally able to catch up with an old friend. Either way, when you first meet someone in person who you've only known online, treat that transitional moment with the same respect and caution you would a new person. While you're already familiar with this person online, being in someone's physical presence is a completely different thing. Read their facial expression and body language for physical cues to help you determine the best way to interact.

There's no doubt we can cultivate meaningful relationships with others through digital communication, but in-person meetings help to strengthen those bonds. As anyone who has tried online dating will tell you, meeting someone in person can be a completely different experience than getting to know them online. Consider these points when balancing your digital and in-person interactions:

Communicate Openly: Ask your new friend or acquaintance what mode of communication they prefer. Some people dislike texting, while others never check their email. Some prefer to speak on the phone or simply meet in person. By asking up front, you'll be able to set the tone and avoid confusion or frustration.

Communicate Intentionally: Set boundaries for the times you will communicate digitally. This is especially important for business relationships, and can often be abused, whether on purpose or unintentionally. Try to keep your digital communications to daylight or during typical working hours, to avoid being intrusive, and also to value your own time.

Communicate Face-to-Face: When possible, meet in person or through telecommunication. This is the best way to assess body language, facial expressions and other micro expressions.

Another aspect to consider is maintaining a professional decorum online, not just between your friends and followers, but in all digital interactions. Some folks don't realize that everything we do can be seen on certain apps and social media sites, from the photos we like to the comments we leave. While there are certain privacy settings that you can employ, nothing is foolproof and you could unintentionally leave someone with an unfavorable impression of you. As we've discussed before, it's also important to set boundaries with people online, including the messages and images you send them. Remember that people consider your online presence during job interviews and when researching potential new friends or love interests.

There's no doubt that we rely on digital communication in the 21st century for just about everything, but it's important to monitor the amount of time we spend online. Taking breaks from digital communication is essential for our overall well-being, so make sure you detox now and then from the online world. Digital burnout is real and could lead you to make social media slip-ups or go down a negative or even dangerous path. Know your limits and log off when needed!

YOUR MISSION

This week, take stock of your online presence. Is your username and email signature professional looking? How about your social media profiles? Do you have everything you need to set up a successful video call? Use this week to pin down how you can brush up your online skills, improve your social media presence and ensure a professional digital footprint.

CONCLUSION

"If you want to be a good conversationalist, be a good listener. To be interesting, be interested."

— DALE CARNEGIE, WORLD-RENOWNED AUTHOR AND LECTURER ON LEADERSHIP

Becoming a successful conversationalist is a lifelong journey; to be truly 'gifted in gab,' I recommend using the techniques in this guide on a regular basis. Times will change, and you'll have to change with them if your goal is to relate and converse with anyone. The good news is that you'll have this guide to return to as needed if you find yourself faltering or need to brush up on certain points. Here is a run-down of what we covered:

Making a Good First Impression: Cultivate your image to put your best foot forward, and be aware of the best ways to present yourself to make a lasting impression.

Captivating Your Audience: Use charisma and charm to capture your listeners' attention and keep it throughout the entire conversation.

Using and Recognizing Body Language: Know the basics of reading others through facial expressions, gestures and body language, and learn how to be aware of your own body language so you can present yourself in the way you want.

Building Rapport: Quickly build rapport, find common ground and connect with others through shared experiences.

Working the Room: Use networking strategies, body language, storytelling and more to turn a roomful of strangers into friends.

Overcoming Challenges: Use communication skills to overcome differences and conversational challenges, and be aware of social cues across cultures.

Encouraging Others: Create a safe space to build trust and practice empathetic listening; use your skills as an empathetic speaker to encourage people to open up to you.

Becoming a Conversational Magnet: Transform yourself into a people magnet with wit, humor and charm; tell funny and interesting stories that will help you leave a lasting impression.

Communicating Effectively Online: Navigate online communication carefully and professionally using email, social media and texting.

As you extend your reach, become more comfortable speaking with others, and meet new people, your skills will grow. Getting out of your shell to speak to new people, many of whom will have different values or are from different backgrounds than you, will only help you improve. Don't pass up business events or turn down invitations to parties. Take every opportunity, from waiting in line for coffee to attending a neighborhood barbecue, to meet someone new. The more you practice talking to others, the more natural it will feel.

I hope this guide will prove to be an excellent start on your journey to learning how to comfortably talk to others, but you should know that it's only the beginning. Seek out experts and watch or listen to their motivational speeches. Be brave and come up with new ways to push yourself out of your comfort zone to build your confidence. Consider taking public speaking classes, if needed, or enroll in acting classes to help you become comfortable with your body language. There are countless ways to continue learning the art of communicating with others, through college courses, at-home learning or good old-fashioned real-life experiences. The key is to keep challenging yourself and make talking to others a priority when appropriate and whenever the opportunity arises.

Being an effective communicator is a super power, and a skill that can help open doors you thought were locked. Learning how to network at events can help you land that dream job or find a position in a whole new industry. Encouraging others to open up to you can help you meet a new friend, or even a romantic love interest. Effective communication plays an essential role in every part of our lives, whether it's negotiating a contract or making sure our doctor really listens to our concerns. Every aspect of our lives — social, personal and professional — depends on being able to talk to others, advocate for ourselves and understand what's going on around us. When we're unable to talk to our fellow humans, we're on a deserted island of our own making, and that is a lonely place to be.

I hope you will take these tips and techniques into account and infuse them into your everyday interactions. Remember, take it one step at a time, one day at a time, one week at a time. Go at your own pace, at your own comfort level, and before you know it, you'll not only be seeking out people to talk to, they'll be seeking out you, as well!

Printed in Great Britain
by Amazon